THESE ARE MY PEOPLE

The Nature of the Church and Its Discipleship According to the New Testament

Harold S. Bender

HERALD PRESS
SCOTTDALE, PENNSYLVANIA

LIBRARY OF CONGRESS CATALOG CARD NUMBER: 62-12947
PRINTED IN THE UNITED STATES OF AMERICA

Unless otherwise indicated all Scripture quotations are from the *Revised Standard Version of the Bible,* copyrighted 1952 by the Division of Christian Education, National Council of Churches, and used by permission.

COPYRIGHT © 1962 BY MENNONITE PUBLISHING HOUSE
SCOTTDALE, PENNSYLVANIA

117932

LIFE Pacific College
Alumni Library
1100 West Covina Blvd.
San Dimas, CA 91773

THESE ARE MY PEOPLE

25.6
132t

LIFE Pacific College
Alumni Library
1100 West Covina Blvd.
San Dimas, CA 91773

To Elizabeth, Mary, and Nancy

L.I.F.E. College Library
1100 Glendale Blvd.
Los Angeles, Calif. 90026

019002

THE CONRAD GREBEL LECTURES

The Conrad Grebel Lectureship was set up for the purpose of making possible an annual study by a Mennonite scholar of some topic of interest and value to the Mennonite Church and to other Christian people. It is administered by a committee appointed by and responsible to the Mennonite Board of Education. This committee appoints the lecturers, approves their subjects, counsels them during their study, and arranges for the delivery of the lectures at one or more places.

The Lectureship is financed by donors who contribute annually $500 each.

Conrad Grebel was an influential leader in the sixteenth-century Swiss Anabaptist movement and is thought of as one of the founders of the Mennonite Church. Because of the direction which he gave to the movement, this Lectureship has been named for him.

Lectures thus far delivered are as follows:

1952–Foundations of Christian Education, by Paul Mininger

1953–Christian Stewardship, by Milo Kauffman

1954–The Way of the Cross in Human Relations, by Guy F. Hershberger

1955–The Alpha and the Omega–A Restatement of the Christian Hope in Christ's Coming, by Paul Erb

1956–The Nurture and Evangelism of Children, by Gideon G. Yoder

1957–The Holy Spirit and the Holy Life, by Chester K. Lehman

1959–The Church Apostolic, by J. D. Graber

1960–These Are My People, by Harold S. Bender

PREFACE

The present volume consists of the Conrad Grebel Lectures for 1960, delivered at Eastern Mennonite College, Goshen College, and Hesston College. I am grateful to the Lectureship Committee which set the theme and gave the commission to write on a topic of major importance as well as one currently the object of much intense interest not only in my own denomination but in Christendom at large. I am grateful also to the committee for its suggestions during the preparation of the lectures, and for the helpful criticism and reactions received from friends who heard or read the lectures, in particular my colleagues in the Associated Mennonite Biblical Seminaries. I am greatly indebted, too, to the many books and articles which have appeared in recent years on the nature of the church and its mission. Specific acknowledgment to certain authors and publishers is made elsewhere in the following pages. I am particularly indebted to my wife Elizabeth and my daughter Mary for their critical reading of the manuscript, from which I have greatly profited.

In content the volume is an essay on the nature of the church as it is understood in the New Testament. As I have sought to describe the church in its true being, I have had ever before me the vision of an identifiable, visible human community, whose nature is determined by its response to the grace of God in Christ. The two poles of God's creative work and man's voluntary response are viewed as essential and reciprocal. The resulting view of the church seems to me to be the one which best reflects both the direct teaching of the New Testament and the performance of the early church. It seeks to avoid the two extremes: on the one hand, a mysticism and theologism which create a picture too remote from the actual experience of the church in history, and on the other hand, the reductionism of a too sociological and humanistic view of the church which would eliminate the work of God in and through its human persons and structures.

The content here offered obviously fails, in more ways than one, to fulfill the promise of the title. The limitation of length owing to the form of five lectures has made the direct treatment of the discipleship of the church brief. This theme deserves a fuller treatment than is possible here, which I hope to give in the not too distant future.

Finally, may I say that the volume is not the essay on the Anabaptist-Mennonite view of the church which some of my readers or even the Lectureship Committee may have expected. However much the content may agree in essence with the Anabaptist view of the church, I have refrained from a historical approach to the material in favor of the approach of New Testament theology. The references to Anabaptism are accordingly brief and without documentation.

It is my hope that the lectures may contribute to the renewal of the church in our day in the image set for it by the New Testament.

Goshen College Biblical Seminary
January, 1962 *Harold S. Bender*

CONTENTS

1

THE PEOPLE OF GOD

On the day of Pentecost one hundred and twenty men of Israel who had responded to Jesus' call to discipleship were together in a house in Jerusalem in the intimate fellowship of prayer and expectation. Assured that the Jesus from whom they had received the commission to make disciples of all the nations was now reigning as Lord over all, they awaited with confidence the descent of the promised Holy Spirit with power.

When the Spirit came they knew that *the day* had come, "the great and manifest day" of the Lord in which salvation would come to whoever would call on His name. Acts 2:21. They knew that they were standing at the turning point of history, when God's redemptive program of the ages was coming to its climax. The "last days"[1] were now come, toward which all God's gracious working since Abraham had been directed. The great promise of God was now being fulfilled in their own experience.

In this great historical setting the one hundred and twenty saw themselves as God's people, the true elect, upon whom the promise for which the covenant people had been chosen and shepherded through the ages was now being bestowed. They knew themselves to be one with the past of God's people, one with the present Messiah, Redeemer, and Lord, one with God's work in the future. They were the bearers of history into a future of untold possibility. The enemy had been overthrown; the way ahead was now clear for the redemption of the race; the kingdom of God had come and the Son of God was reigning, seated on the throne of authority. Acts 2:20. Israel's missionary assignment had been fulfilled in Christ, and transferred by Him to them. Henceforth, God would work through them to accomplish His purpose of gathering out of all the nations a people for His name.

The one hundred and twenty, and all whom God would add to them, were now the people of God, in continuity with the people of the Abrahamic and Sinaitic covenants, yet living under the new covenant established by the sacrifice of the blood of the Redeemer in a new relationship to God through Christ. Now race no longer counted, if indeed it ever did, only a faith-relationship to Christ. Nor were there now two parallel peoples of God, the new and the old, to go down through history side by side forever. There was only one people, the new people of God. Those of the historical nation of Israel who would not repent and believe in Christ were of "the crooked generation," with no part in the new Israel. "Save yourselves from this crooked generation," said Peter; "repent and believe, and you shall receive the promise" which was intended for you, and you shall be incorporated into the people of God by the Holy Spirit; but until then you are the lost generation.[2] Thus the breach with the idea of an ethnic Israel was clear, even though the new Israel continued certain cultural practices of the old Israel and joined for a time with it in the hours of prayer in the temple.

Thus was fulfilled the judgment that Jesus in His Messianic office had pronounced upon the Jewish nation: "The kingdom of God will be taken away from you and given to a nation producing the fruits of it" (Matt. 21:43). Paul understood this clearly, as he stated in his epistle to the Romans, chapters 9 to 11: "But of [the old] Israel he says, 'All day long I have held out my hands to a disobedient and contrary people' " (10:21). God had not rejected His people, said Paul; He had simply gone forward with the "remnant, chosen by grace," for "the elect obtained it, but the rest were hardened" (11:5, 7). This remnant of grace was the church of Pentecost and after, and Paul identified himself with this remnant. The old branches, he says, "were broken off [by God] because of their unbelief" (11:20), although the main trunk of the tree, that is, the basic people of God, was continued. The new branches were grafted into this trunk and henceforth were to be the only branches on the tree, until, at some later time, the old branches would be grafted in again. 11:24.

Paul, like Peter at Pentecost, was keenly aware that the climax in the history of God's people had come. He made it clear to the Gentile believers that they too were a part of the historic and now new people of God. It was the Galatians whom he called "the Israel of God" (Galatians 6:16). It was to the Corinthians that he said, "the end of the ages has come" (I Corinthians 10:11), that is, the goal toward which the divine redemptive plan had been moving through the ages. It was to the Ephesians that he said, "he chose us in him before the foundation of the world. . . . He destined us in love to be his sons" (Ephesians 1:4, 5). The Gentiles had been "alienated from the commonwealth of Israel, and strangers to the covenants of promise. . . . But now . . . you who once were far off have been brought near in the blood of Christ . . . who has made us both one, . . . one body through the cross, thereby bringing the hostility to an end. . . . So then you are no longer strangers and sojourners, but . . . fellow citizens . . . and members of the household of God, . . . a holy temple in the Lord; in whom you also are built into it for a dwelling place of God in the Spirit" (Ephesians 2:12-22). In these great affirmations Paul makes clear that those among the Gentiles who believe are incorporated into the people of God on a fully equal basis with those Israelites who believe. The commonwealth of Israel, the household of God, is now to be composed of believers in Christ of all races and cultures. "Here there cannot be Greek and Jew" (Colossians 3:11), for there is no longer an ethnic people of God, only a spiritual people of God, because "Christ is all, and in all." The "new people" of God are of course under the new covenant and order with a new mode of organization and administration, a new standard of ethics, a new relationship to the world, and new resources in Christ and the Holy Spirit for their life under the lordship of Christ.

This identification of the disciples[3] of Christ as the people of God is further confirmed by the name which the new people of God gave to themselves, that is, the "church," in Greek the *ecclesia*.[4] First used by Christ twice in Matthew 16 and 18, then by Luke twenty-one times in his history of the apostolic church in Acts, by Paul sixty-two times in eleven of his epistles, by John twenty times in the Revelation, and six times by three other writers (only the epistles of Peter and Jude being without this word), it appears at least 110 times in the New Testament. It is by far the most common direct designation of the body of believers. It is used freely and indiscriminately to refer to the universal church on earth or in heaven, the local body of believers meeting in a small assembly in a house, all the thousands in a city like Jerusalem, or the collective local congregations in a province like Syria or Cilicia. When used for a local meeting group it is thought of as a manifestation of the general church, for the general church is prior to the local expression of it. But the chief point to be made here is that it is used with the deliberate intent to identify the church as the people of God, continuous with the faithful people of God in pre-Pentecost and Old Testament times. This is not to imply that the Old Testament term *ecclesia* has the same content as the word when used in the New Testament; there are significant differences. The only point made here is that in both Testaments the first and essential meaning is the same, namely that a given historic group stands in such a relationship to God as to belong to Him as His people.

The history of the usage of the word *ecclesia* makes this clear. Outside the New Testament it had no religious connotation at all, its universal meaning in the Greco-Roman world being that of an assembly of citizens in a city. But in the Greek translation of the Old Testament, the Septuagint, which Paul and most of the early Christians used as their Bible and from which are taken more than half the quotations from the Old Testament found in the New Testament, it appears some eighty times, always with a religious meaning.[5] In all but three cases it is the translation of the Hebrew term for the whole community of Israel as the people of God, the word *qahal*. Another Hebrew word, *edhah,* was also used in the Hebrew Old Testament to refer to much the same idea, but almost all of its occurrences are early, in the Pentateuch only. *Qahal* gradually displaced *edhah,* and after the Exile became the almost exclusive term for the people of God, either in local assembly or in the absolute sense of all Israel. Although in the

Pentateuch "synagogue" is frequently used to translate *qahal,* after Deuteronomy 5:10 *ecclesia* is the customary translation. Sometimes the expression for people of God is *Jehovah qahal,* Jehovah being placed first to give strong emphasis to God's possession of His people. For this the Greek translation is *ecclesia kuriou,* the "church of the Lord," that is, "the church of God." In the New Testament this very expression "church of God" or "churches of God" is frequently used, especially by Paul, and even when the word *ecclesia* stands alone, omitting the phrase "of God," it is to be understood as "of God," just as "kingdom" is always to be understood as "kingdom of God," whether standing alone or with the added phrase "of God." The word *ecclesia* often stands alone, both singular and plural, sometimes with and sometimes without the definite article, for it became in effect a proper name. All the Jewish Christians understood that *ecclesia* meant the people of God. It must have been equally clear to the Gentile believers, to whom Paul certainly conveyed this meaning. The best translation of *ecclesia* is really "people of God." Such a translation would emphasize its essential meaning and avoid some modern false or uncertain connotations connected with the word "church."

The identification of the disciples of Jesus as the covenant people of God, the ongoing bearers of the promise and of the redeeming grace of God, is further supported by the New Testament application to the church of a multitude of other terms applied to Israel in the Old Testament. I use here Paul Minear's listing of such terms in his *Images of the Church in the New Testament*:[6] "a holy nation, the twelve tribes, the circumcision, the fathers and their descendants, sons of Abraham, the exodus pilgrims, the house of David, the remnant, the elect." In addition to these terms which apply to Israel as a whole, analogies or metaphors drawn from the worship of Israel are also applied to the church in the New Testament; again Minear's listing: "Jerusalem, sometimes called simply *the* city but also the *Holy* City, the City of *David;* Mount Zion and the temple located there; the priesthood and its work; the sacrifices presented by the worshipers, including the aroma or sweet savor of the sacrifice; the festivals and holy days, such as Pentecost and Passover." Also the central image of the high-priestly work of Christ with the sacrifice of Christ and the figure of the Lamb, upon which the church is founded, is of course taken directly from the Old Testament. The church appropriated all these images for itself because it understood itself to stand in the direct spiritual succession of the Old Testament faith. The Old Testament system of ceremonies and cult forms was abolished, but their spiritual meaning was continued.

Note further that Peter and others plainly named the body of believers the people of God. Though never using the word *ecclesia* in his epistles, Peter states most explicitly the idea that the body of believers is the continuing people of God. "But you are a chosen race, a royal priesthood, a holy nation, God's own people. . . . Once you were no people but now you are God's people; once you had not received mercy but now you have received mercy" (I Peter 2:9, 10). The last phrase is important because the true and chief mark of the people of God in all ages is that they are the recipients of God's mercy which produces life and response in them. Paul's use of the terms "Israel" (Galatians 6:16) and "commonwealth of Israel" (Ephesians 2:12, 19) for the church has already been noted; at one place he even calls the church "the true circumcision" (Philippians 3:3). The writer of Hebrews refers to the church as "the house of Israel" and "my people" (Hebrews 8:8, 10), applying to it the prophecy of Jeremiah 31:31-34.

The evidence assembled above regarding the identification of the church with God's people of the old covenant not only suggests that the Old Testament is necessary to understand the New Testament, particularly the church. Beyond that it calls for a clear understanding of the unity of the two Testaments as the Word of God. The Biblical concept of the continuing people of God under one God, with one purpose of God throughout, requires this understanding. This does not mean that there is nothing new in the new covenant, for there is indeed about the people of God as found in the church something marvelously new and better in the new age, for there is in Christ the fullness of divine revelation. In Him there is the completed work of redemption, and grace upon grace. The old covenant is annulled, superseded by the new; the old law has passed away. This newness will be the theme of the second chapter where the church is displayed as the body of Christ. But God's work in the world and in history does not begin with the New Testament, nor do His people begin there. He always had a people, from Abraham on down.[7] To be sure His work in and through the church began at Pentecost, and we may call the new age the dispensation of grace in contrast to the old dispensation of law. But in no case dare we imperil the grace of God under the old covenant, for grace did not begin with Pentecost, it only assumed a new form.

Some may now be asking, How can believers in Christ be in succession to the Old Testament people of God, who were the biologically distinct Hebrew race, the literal sons of Abraham through Isaac and Jacob, an ethnic group rigidly separate from all other ethnic groups, whereas the church is no ethnic group but is universal in character? Furthermore the Hebrews had a national political structure in the form of a theocracy, whereas the church has no political form, for Jesus broke through Jewish particularism, saying "make disciples of all nations," "preach the gospel to every creature." Paul said emphatically that neither circumcision nor uncircumcision counts for anything. Galatians 6:15.

The answer to this question requires no forcing of meanings of either Old or New Testament, but a proper interpretation of both, particularly of the Old Testament.

The first key to the proper solution of this problem is the key furnished by Paul in his insistence that no Old Testament saint was ever saved or made acceptable to God by works of the law, not even Abraham. All who were saved in the past were saved by faith, not by membership in an ethnic group. The ceremonial law had only teaching value through its symbolism; it never had operative value as a sacramental system. In this connection the sharp condemnation by the prophets of those who trusted in ceremonies, but whose hearts were far from God, comes to mind. Isaiah 29:13; Joel 2:13, *et al.* The sacrifices of a broken and contrite heart were the only true sacrifices, the psalmist said. Psalm 51:16, 17. It was only the circumcision of the heart that counted, says Paul. Romans 2:28. John the Baptist warned his generation, "Do not presume to say to yourselves, 'We have Abraham as our father.' . . . Bear fruit that befits repentance" (Matthew 3:8, 9). Jesus in a similar way challenged the same generation when they claimed to be sons of Abraham. "If you were Abraham's children, you would do what Abraham did" (John 8:39). And Paul told the Galatians, "It is men of faith who are the sons of Abraham. . . . For all who rely on works of the law are under a curse" (Galatians 3:7, 10). And again (Galatians 3:29), "If you are Christ's, then you are Abraham's offspring, heirs according to promise." Or again (Romans 9:6, 8), "For not all who are descended from Israel belong to Israel. . . . This means that it is not the children of the flesh who are the children of God," and he is a Jew who is one inwardly. "For he is not a real Jew who is one outwardly . . ." (Romans 2:28, 29).

Nor may we say that these denials of the value of biological descent from Abraham were only intended for the saints of the New Testament. This is not only New Testament doctrine; it was as true in the days of Abraham or of the prophets or of the psalmists as in Paul's day—true always and everywhere. The Israelites prior to Christ did not enjoy the blessings of God because they were Jews or Semites, nor because they were sons of Abraham after the flesh, but because God had chosen them and bestowed His love upon them. Nor were they the people of God because they kept the law and offered sacrifices, or because they maintained racial segregation. They did these things because God had made a covenant with them and thus made them His people out of free grace and sovereign election, and had given them the pattern of their religious and social life. Jews after the flesh have never had a claim upon God's grace, past, present, or future. Their only claim is one based upon the covenant, which is a relationship after the spirit.

But there is another consideration that must be noted. Historically, by no means were all Jews after the flesh Jews after the spirit. Nor were they all really the people of God, even though they practiced circumcision and racial purity. The true people of God were always the spiritual people, not the biological people, and they were a remnant, produced by God's judgment and grace.[8] Only a part of the ethnic group were the people of God, for a major part was always in spiritual apostasy. This is the picture of Israel as presented in the Old Testament by both historical writers and prophets. The prophets sought by their warnings and promises to lead more of ethnic Israel to become spiritual Israel, but it was only the remnant which ultimately was God's true Israel. This Old Testament doctrine of the remnant becomes ever more clear as the old dispensation wears out. It was not merely that only the spiritual remnant would be saved while the main body was apostate and cast off. The saved remnant was to be the saving remnant, who would bring salvation to their nation and the nations. It was this remnant then which became the church, the "present time . . . remnant, chosen by grace," which Paul identified in Romans 11:5.

Again, it should be noted that the law and the sacrificial system were not of the essence of the people of God. Neither was the political state, the dynasty of David, the city of Jerusalem, nor the land of Palestine of the essence. These all were a consequence of the covenant and the promise, serving as a means to an end, and are not to be absolutized. They were not absolutized in the Old Testament. None of these guaranteed the spiritual reality of the people of God, being only aids to it; and all of them failed at one time or another. The dynasty of David was wiped out; for centuries before Christ the throne of David was vacant, until Greater David came to reign. The tabernacle of David had fallen down, says James, and was being re-erected in the new age out of its ruins. Acts 15:13-17. The political state of Israel-Judah disappeared, not to be restored until 1947. And the modern state of Israel is not the Israel of faith. In the Babylonian captivity the very nation and ethnic group was destroyed, and its land taken over by foreign rulers who not only took much of the population as slaves to regions 300 miles and more away, but who even introduced foreign non-Jewish settlers into the land to create a racial mixture. In the days of Jesus the Jewish people were maintained not by national political independence but by a cultural and religious leadership. It was the Pharisees, the scribes, the Sanhedrin, the elders of the synagogues, who kept ethnic Israel alive, while the Greek conquerors and later the Romans occupied the land and ruled the people. But these also failed to maintain the remnant as the spiritual people of God. Ethnic and cultural Israel was always only the shell within which the true Israel was enclosed and nurtured. To be sure, spiritual Israel was always a part of ethnic Israel and outwardly integrated into it, under the shell.

Further, when the great day of the Lord came at Pentecost, no new and better ethnic Israel, no new and better sacrificial system, no new national or political structure was established. In fact, all this was superseded by the new and better provision in Christ (see *Hebrews*). When the temptation came to Jesus in the wilderness to act politically, He rejected it. Paul's hope for the future of racial Israel was that they would be saved spiritually by coming to faith in Christ, not by a restoration of the national state and Jewish culture. He makes it clear in Ephesians as John does in Revelation that the church is never to be displaced as the people of God by ethnic Israel; for to God will be given "glory in the church and in Christ Jesus to all generations, for ever and ever" (Ephesians 3:21). The destruction of Jerusalem and the temple in A.D. 70 was rightly seen by the Christians of that day as the final judgment of God upon an unbelieving and unrepentant national Israel who had rejected the Messiah. The church is not the continuation of ethnic Israel but of spiritual Israel. Ethnic Israel continued, but outside of God's plan.

The evident historical rejection and elimination of national and ethnic Israel from the plan of God, which made room for the new creation, was not the only reason, or even the major reason, why the church could feel itself to be the people of God. Just as the people of God were constituted in a special way by the mighty acts of God in the exodus from Egypt and the covenant at Sinai, so the new people of God were constituted by the mighty acts of God in the incarnation of Christ, His works, His death, and His resurrection, and by the descent of the Holy Spirit with power at Pentecost. These acts they had seen and experienced. They knew that God was again at work now, acting, creating, transforming, manifesting Himself in gathering a people for His name. Had not Jesus told His disciples, "I will build my church"? And when there was hesitancy in the apostolic church about the extension of the boundary of the people of God beyond those of Jewish ethnic background the convincing factor was the direct action of God in sending the Holy Spirit upon those in Samaria who believed under Philip's preaching, as well as later upon Cornelius and his household, together with the direct and specific command of God to Peter in his vision in Joppa to accept Cornelius. The report of Paul and Barnabas to the Jerusalem Council relating "what signs and wonders God had done through them among the Gentiles" (Acts 15:7-9, 12) was what convinced the Council to move forward in its resolution of the problem of the unity of Gentiles and Jews in the church. Again, as Minear[9] and others have pointed out, the early church thought of itself as engaged in a great "exodus of salvation," coming out of spiritual bondage into the promised land of God's saved people, quite in the analogy of the historical exodus from Egypt of old into the promised land of Palestine. It was God's new mighty works which made possible this new exodus and accompanied the pilgrims along the way to their ultimate goal of the heavenly city of God, the new Mount Zion. In both the Old and New Testament idea of the people of God, the essential is that God chooses and creates His people, and that they become His people by responding to His gracious acts.

Having noted the historical identification of the church as the people of God, beginning at Pentecost, it remains to examine theologically the meaning of this identification for the understanding of the nature of the church.

The first implication of the concept is that the church is a company of concrete living persons in the flesh, living in time and space, though no longer bound to one geographic area. It is a visible identifiable human company, not an invisible, mystical phenomenon. It is the counterpart of visible Old Testament Israel. This is true even though it is the counterpart only to the remnant spiritual Israel, not to the shell of ethnic Israel. The spiritual Israelites were still visible and identifiable as servants of God.

The second implication of the concept is that the church is called into being by God Himself. As in the Old Testament, so in the new day God's purpose and action come first. His people emerge as an expression of His prior purpose, and are therefore an expression of grace. "Everywhere in the Bible," says Minear, "we hear the assertion that the birth and survival of this people are due alone to God's gracious and faithful action in creating, calling, sustaining, judging, and saving it. They are a people only because He dwells within them and moves among them."[10] They are a people because He offered a covenant to those who were to become His people, which they accepted. They are a people because of His sovereign election, not by their own choice or endeavor. Just so the New Testament church comes into existence by the gracious act of God in Christ. The new covenant is offered in the blood of Christ. The church is created by God's mighty acts, and she continues to exist only because God dwells in her midst—she is His temple. The new people are the elect.

Thus, the church never can be thought of as a merely human institution created as a voluntary compact by human beings interested in religion, even in the religion of Jesus. She owes her life to God, and all those who are added to her are added by God. Acts 2:47. The church's point of reference is always transcendent, outside herself.

Furthermore, God determines the boundaries of eligibility for membership in His people. Unfortunately, the people of both the Old and the New Testament and beyond have often fallen into the temptation of fixing their own eligibility boundaries on racial or cultural bases, excluding whom they will. When they do this, they forget that "Those who were not my people I will call 'my people,' and her who was not beloved I will call 'my beloved.' And in the very place where it was said to them, 'You are not my people,' they will be called 'sons of the living God' " (Romans 9:25, 26). This in no sense denies the obligation of God's people to fix the spiritual requirements for membership or to fix the boundaries of separation from the world. It merely means that the church can fix for itself no ethnic, national, or cultural boundaries.

We have noted that the people of God are His people by His choice and election. But this is to be understood basically as an election of a people, not an election of individuals.[11] God has determined in advance that He will have a people; He has predestined the church; this is absolute. The election of individuals to be in this church is conditioned upon their response. The determination of which individuals become members of the people of God is dependent upon the individual response, not the fiat of God. God wills that all should be saved, but only whosoever will will be saved. Individuals come and go, but the people of God go on forever. On the basis of the principle that ethnic character has no significance for God and that therefore the retention of ethnic groups or individuals is not necessary, the continuity between the old and the new people of God can be understood, even though there was discontinuity when ethnic Israel refused in large measure to accept the Messiah.

Another major facet of the meaning of the concept of the people of God is that they are the people who respond to God.[12] His is the initiative of grace, His the approach; He acts to elect and call a people; He saves and sustains His people. But they come into existence only by a response on their part. Abraham did not choose his call or destination, but he had to follow the call and leave his country and kindred, or God could not have used him. The covenant was not effective at Sinai until Israel responded and pledged its allegiance and obedience solely to God. The later loss of covenant rights and privileges by Israel was the result of its disobedience, disloyalty, and unbelief; it was not an arbitrary act on God's part. The Messiah rejected the Jews, His own people, because they rejected Him and did not bring forth the fruits of the kingdom. John 1:11; Matthew 21:43. The relation of Israel to God was always conditioned upon their response, even though this basic truth may not always be mentioned on every occasion of the mention of the covenant relationship or the promise.[13] As Israel, so is the church. The church came into existence likewise in response to God, by repentance and faith. The church does not exist apart from believing in Christ; it is a believing people. The Holy Spirit comes only upon those who believe. The offer of salvation is indeed made by God, but the acceptance is an act of the responder.

Further, response to God's grace is not only the initial act to establish relationship; it is a needed continuing action in the life of the church to maintain the relationship. This is illustrated by the many ways in which the New Testament speaks of the church. The members of the church are disciples, followers, confessors, believers, witnesses, ambassadors, pilgrims, stewards, ministers, faithful ones—all terms connoting response and activity by the members. In all these ways of speaking, the New Testament constantly reminds us that in whatever exalted language the church is spoken of as the people of God from the point of view of God's gracious acting, the church is a concrete community of human persons who are nevertheless expected to respond to God, and who exist only when they do so respond.

This understanding is further supported by the observation that the exalted assertions about what God does in His grace are intermingled with exhortations to response. It is the mercies of God which are the ground of the appeal by Paul, but it is the human members of the church who are called upon to present bodies and minds as the living response of sacrifice. Romans 12:1, 2. And the appeal is not incidental, it is necessary; not only because the Roman Christians may have been weak in their response, but to bring out the essential need for a response, and the right basis for it.

The church can refuse its response or give an inadequate response, but in so doing it diminishes or destroys itself. The church can, like Israel, become disobedient, unbelieving, and apostate, because the response is its free choice and responsibility, and in its humanity it is not infallible. God's grace does not compel or guarantee the church's response. In this respect the new Israel is precisely like the old Israel. But the difference between the church of the new age and ethnic Israel is that entrance into the people of God is by a personal decision of the individual. Men are added to the church as they respond to the preaching of the Gospel, not by ethnic birth and physical marking. Membership in the remnant spiritual Israel was, of course, on the basis of personal response and commitment.

It is this difference that requires the abandonment of any attempt to substitute a nonvoluntary form of entrance into the church, such as infant baptism, for the Old Testament rite of circumcision. Even under the old covenant circumcision of the heart was necessary, and this required voluntary faith. Members of the church cannot be born into the church biologically; they must choose to enter it. To be sure, the advocates of infant baptism claim that the ceremony symbolizes the prior act of God's grace in providing salvation, but they forget that any ceremony of admission into the church, while it does this, must at the same time represent man's free believing response. This baptism in infancy cannot do. The infant is *compelled* by others to enter the church; it is not his *choice,* and it is freely conceded that he cannot have faith in the New Testament sense. Nor can the response of others be substituted for the personal response of the individual without denying the meaning of responsible response. Seen in this light, to practice infant baptism is to deny the New Testament understanding of the church. This logical conclusion is further supported by the fact that the early church did not practice infant baptism, as has been conclusively shown by Kurt Aland in a recent study.[14]

This basic understanding of the church as a responding people of God is well stated by Welch in his *The Reality of the Church.* "The church may be fully dependent on God's act, but it is not simply God acting. It is a people believing, worshiping, obeying, witnessing."[15] To say that the church is divine and not human is to deny this very obvious fact. The church is God's divine creation indeed, but it cannot exist without the human response of faith. It may exist without you or me, but it cannot exist without *anyone*, as Welch says.

The concept of a responding people has a further implication, namely, that of the visibility of the church. The experience of the mercy of God to the individual and that individual's response, that is, the relationship of the believer to Christ, is an inner experience, but the individual is an identifiable visible person. The New Testament knows of no invisible church. As Karl Ludwig Schmidt has said, "The church is as visible as the Christian man."[16] There must be public confession of Christ with the mouth and with the life. The "churches of God" are indeed "in Christ," but they are also "in Judea." The body of Christ is not a *mere* fellowship of men, but it *is* a fellowship of men. There are mysteries in the realm of God's dealing with men, but the manifestation of the results of this dealing is not secret; it is open and known to men. It is true that Christ confronts man in the Gospel, but this Gospel comes to man in the witness of the living visible church.

Believers are to love the invisible God with all their being, but this must find expression in the love of the very human and visible neighbor. I John 4:20; Luke 10:27. Indeed, John says in his epistle that this love of the needy neighbor is the test of loving God. I John 4:20. The incarnation of God in the flesh is paralleled by the incarnation of the church in a concrete human community. The doctrine of the invisible church is the invention of the Reformers, who wished to maintain the mass church of the medieval centuries in its visible structure while at the same time protecting their doctrine of justification by faith as an essential mark of the Christian believer. By this construction they evaded the necessity of rejecting the mass of Christians who were in reality "outside" of Christ, while rejecting the Catholic view that all were saved.

We affirm then the dual nature of the church. It is indeed called by God, but it responds to Him as a human community which lives out in time and space the life which comes from above.

A footnote from church history is appropriate here concerning the Anabaptists of the Reformation period who sought to be the true church of Christ after the New Testament pattern, and who consequently rejected the mass church of the Reformers for the believers' church. They could have spared themselves untold suffering at the hands of the persecuting state churches had they been willing to suspend the creation of visible churches committed in full obedience to Christ. There were those who did this, preeminently the Spiritualists of their day, Caspar Schwenckfeld and others. But the very heart of the Anabaptist commitment to Christ was to follow Him openly in life. The new life in Christ was to be in evidence, wrought out in the human relations of the concrete social order. There was to be no crypto-discipleship in the private retreat of contemplation. Nor was there to be any surrender to the life standards of the world by a retreat into justification by faith. Christ was to be made visible in the church, and the church was to be made visible in the world, whatever the cost. This the Anabaptists conceived to be the original apostolic pattern of the church as given in the New Testament, and they viewed themselves as restoring this pattern, and thus completing the Reformation.[17] The Anabaptists offer thus an illustration of an alternate pattern of the church to the one which developed as a result of the Constantinian compromise and was continued in state church Protestantism.

The emphasis upon the humanness and visible historical character of the church gives rise to the legitimate question whether the empirical historical church has been the true church of Christ. We can scarcely claim that all historical manifestations of the church conform to the nature of the church of Christ as set forth in this chapter thus far, or as it will be set forth in the succeeding chapters. Upon reviewing the history of the professed church of Christ some have despaired of realizing the true church in history and have accepted the conclusion that the true church can only be thought of as the invisible company of true believers, inside the shell of the professing church, which is known only to God. They have therefore recommended abandoning the attempt to identify or even produce the true church. *Ecclesiola in ecclesia,* little true church in the big nominal church, becomes then an alternate. They say: Let us give up the ideal, since practically we cannot guarantee that the empirical church is the true church. In such a view the church becomes more like a hospital than a temple, with a mixed multitude of sinners and saints as its membership.

Jesus Himself faced the problem and resolved it. He said, "Not every one who says to me, 'Lord, Lord,' shall enter the kingdom of heaven" (Matthew 7:21), and He insisted that men shall be known by their fruits. He admitted that there will be non-fruit-bearing branches on the vine, which must be cut off (John 15:2), but He did not for that reason abandon His program of establishing His kingdom on earth. Nor may we, His followers, surrender in the attempt to build the ideal obedient church because there will be some human failure. It is our assignment to preach the Gospel, invite free response, accept as sincere the confession of repentance and faith of the candidate for membership, and incorporate him into the visible fellowship for nurture. It may become necessary to exclude from the visible fellowship those whose "Lord, Lord" turns out to be insincere and who fail to bear fruit. For although their eternal destiny is in the hands of Christ, the righteous Judge, their temporal status is one of unbelief outside the fold of Christ. Any other course is to make the visible church the counterpart of ethnic Israel containing within itself the hidden remnant of faith; but this is not the people of God of the new covenant. The church must be built visibly in the midst of a broken world as the expression of God's redemption in Christ.

2

THE BODY OF CHRIST

THE figure of the church as the body of Christ is one of the most striking and significant of all the figures applied to the church in the New Testament. It carries such a weight of meaning that it becomes an indispensable category for the understanding of the nature of the church. It corresponds to the figure of the vine and the branches which Jesus Himself used to represent His relationship to His people. It carries in image the whole of Christian experience, from the initial act of repentance to final redemption, and also much of the idea of membership in the church. It is widely used in Christian thought, and among some has come to be the dominant image of the church, or at least the prior image around which all others are grouped and by which all others are interpreted.[1]

But to make this figure unduly central is not to see the New Testament doctrine of the church in proper balance. Minear has pointed out that over eighty images and analogies of the church are found in the New Testament, some of them of great importance, such as the image of the people of God, which we have considered in the first chapter. This latter image has priority to the image of the body, both in the historical experience of the church and in logic, in that it expounds the relation of the church to God, whereas the image of the body of Christ represents the relation to Christ, the Son. Nor is the idea of "body" carried in the name *ecclesia.* "Body" is an exclusively Pauline concept, found only in five books—Romans, I and II Corinthians, Ephesians, and Colossians,[2] and though used there in a very weighty sense, it is by no means the most frequent figure of the church found in the New Testament. Let us examine the meaning of the image, not forgetting that it does not exhaust the nature of the church.

Two additional figures are connected with Paul's use of the image of the body, namely, that of the head of the body and that of the members of the body. These are independent figures as Paul uses them and not derivative from the idea of the body, though they are often interwoven with it in such a way as to appear to be one, and though they logically might seem to be involved in the body. Paul's thought oscillates among the three, moving back and forth without hesitation from one aspect or meaning to another. Sometimes the stress is on the subjection of the body to the head, sometimes on the responsibility of the members to one another, sometimes on the unity of the body, sometimes on the growth of the body through what the members supply, and at other times on growth by receiving life and nourishment from the head. These are only ways of conveying truth about the church; hence, it is not necessary to force them all into one systematic whole. When we do use this Pauline material somewhat systematically to understand the nature of the church, we must remember that Paul was not discoursing on the nature of the church, but addressing himself to concrete situations and dealing with needs and problems of individual empirical congregations. We should also be careful not to force logical consequences out of this analogy which are not stated or at least implied, a temptation to Bible interpreters in all types of figurative language.

The image of the body of Christ speaks first of all of the centrality of *Christ* in the life of the church; the emphasis in the phrase is on the word "Christ." Whereas the image of the people of God drew our attention to the history of redemption through the ages and to God's mighty works at the climax of that history at Calvary and Pentecost, the phrase "body of Christ" emphasizes the immediate contemporary living relationship of Christ to the church, including, of course, the relationship to the historic Christ of Calvary. God was in Christ and is in Christ, to be sure; the two images, people of God and body of Christ, are inseparable; but the main thrust of the second image is that the life of the church since the resurrection is to be understood as wholly dependent upon Christ, as the living human body is dependent upon its source of life. The inseparability of the church from Christ is asserted in vivid and powerful metaphors. If the church languishes or is sickly it is because it is "not holding fast to the Head, from whom the whole body, nourished and knit together . . . , grows with a growth that is from God" (Colossians 2:19). The body grows just because it is Christ's body. "We are to grow up in every way into him who is the head, into Christ, from whom the whole body . . . makes bodily growth and upbuilds itself in love" (Ephesians 4:15, 16). This utter dependence and close intimacy between Christ and the church is also expressed in other figures by Paul, particularly in the transcendent phrase "in Christ," or its counterpart "Christ in us," or the idea of union with Christ. Indeed, the concept "in Christ" must be understood to be behind the phrase "body of Christ" and carrying it. Here we stand therefore at the very heart of the Christian faith. God's act creates His people, who live in Christ. Neither image is independent of the other nor subordinate to it, although one is prior. Both are united in the unity of the Godhead.

As we seek to fathom its depth of meaning, we must remember that the content in the figure of the body cannot be found by logical deductions from the modern concept "body." It must be derived rather from an examination of the background of the Biblical and Hebraic usage of the term and from the various contexts in which the phrase appears in the New Testament. To this examination we now proceed.

Behind the image of the body is the Hebrew notion of corporate personality.[3] The pronounced individualism of our Western culture today, resting as it does upon Greek thought, makes it difficult for us fully to grasp this idea. For the Hebrew the individual existed only as a particular expression of the total people; his character was determined by solidarity with all others of his people. His people were prior to himself as an individual. This sense of solidarity with a group underlies Paul's use of the figures of the first and the second Adam to explain sin and redemption, "For as in Adam all die, so also in Christ shall all be made alive" (I Corinthians 15:22). The same concept is the key to the understanding of such passages as those in Romans 6, where Paul speaks of burial with Christ and resurrection with Him. "For if we have been united with him in a death like his, we shall certainly be united . . . in a resurrection like his" (Romans 6:5). "But if we have died with Christ, we believe that we shall also live with him" (Romans 6:8). To "*live with* Christ" is not to *be with* Him, spatially or temporally, or merely to have fellowship with Him, but to be in solidarity with Him so that His life is our life, for we are to be one body with Him. We can use the word "fellowship" for this relationship if we really mean it in the New Testament sense of *koinonia,* which always carries the sense of sharing, of participating in a common life, rather than the mere "togetherness" which our modern social usage has given to it.

In the light of this understanding we can see more clearly the meaning of the two humanities in Pauline teaching, the old man and the new man.[4] All human beings belong first of all to the old man, the first Adam, by whose sin death entered into all men, since the race is one in solidarity. This sinful humanity is described as the "body of death." In other words, the human situation apart from Christ is one of death—death for one and all. "Who will deliver me from this body of death?" Paul exclaims (Romans 7:24), meaning, "How shall I escape from the sinful humanity with which I am in solidarity, of which I am an inextricable part?" The answer comes clearly. "As by *a man* came death, by *a man* has come also the resurrection of the dead," that is, the deliverance. I Corinthians 15:21. As the destiny of men is determined by their solidarity with the first and sinful Adam and all his race, so the destiny of men can be changed if they become a part of the new man, Jesus Christ, in full solidarity with Him and His new race. This new destiny is "the free gift" of God, which leads to "acquittal and life for all men" (Romans 5:18) and to the "reign in life through the one man Jesus Christ" (Romans 5:17). Paul's complicated figure of dying in order to be delivered from death is easily comprehended if we keep in mind the two solidarities of which man is a part. Dying with Christ is the second solidarity; it means life because the dying Christ will rise out of death, bringing with Him all who are in solidarity with Him by faith.

The first meaning, then, of the "body of Christ" is that redemption from the body of death (sin) comes through being in the living body of Christ (the church). Redemption is transfer from one body to another. God makes the transfer, conditioned upon faith-solidarity with Christ. "Brethren, you have died to the law through the body of Christ, so that you may belong to another, to him who has been raised from the dead in order that we may bear fruit for God" (Romans 7:4). Two solidarities are open to men, the two bodies to one of which every man belongs. The first is universal; all men belong to it before redemption. The second can become universal, though each man must decide his destiny alone, and enters the new body by his response to God's initiative. They are mutually exclusive, for they are two antithetical conflicting realms, two warring kingdoms. Christian believers have all been transferred out of the first body to the second, with vast consequences. They have been delivered from the bondage of the old man and now have a new "belongingness," and a new function to bear fruit for God. This transfer is the fundamental experience which is essential for the existence of the church; it is a basic category of New Testament thought. It is repeated in several other figures, such as the one of the two kingdoms, as in Colossians (1:13), where the same truth is expressed in the passage which defines redemption as being transferred from the "dominion of darkness . . . to the kingdom of his beloved Son." In the same chapter of Colossians Paul swings back again into the figure of the body, describing redemption as being "now reconciled in his body of flesh by his death" (verse 22). It is essential to remember that Paul's vision of this transfer is not primarily of individuals, though effective for them, but of the whole church as the totality of believers.

It will be observed that in these Scripture passages there are varieties of meaning in the use of the term "body." At one time the body of Christ may mean the new humanity, that is, the church, at another the Christ whose body was nailed on the tree, at another the Christ of the resurrection body, and at still another time the specific person who is a participant in one of the two solidarities described above. The most involved aspect of the body concept is the solidarity of the believer with Christ's dying body and then with His risen body, where the body "of the flesh" and the body of spiritual life "in him" are strangely united in one reality. This is possible, of course, because it is the same Christ carrying His saving work through the whole act of redemption, from the descent of the incarnation and Calvary, and through the resurrection and exaltation back to glory. Another shade of meaning of "body" is found in the declarations that specifically imply the church on earth. "We were all baptized into one body" (I Corinthians 12:13), and again, "there is one body and one Spirit" (Ephesians 4:4). The body here means both the spiritual body and the visible church.

For many the concept of being a part of the body of Christ or being "in Christ" is difficult to comprehend. It seems to be something mystical and mysterious, or it sounds like mere theologizing; it conveys no sense of reality. Yet it is difficult to exaggerate the importance of this idea for Paul and the church. It appears in all his letters and is used almost constantly. Paul asserts that Christians are now "in Christ," not just striving to be in Him, or hoping sometime to become worthy to be in Him. In fact, being a Christian means being in Christ; there is no Christian outside of Christ; there is no church outside of Christ. What then does Paul mean by this expression?

Here I follow Welch as he seeks to make its meaning clear in his recent book, *The Reality of the Church.*[5]

To be in Christ means, first of all, to receive what God has done in the historic Christ, for God was in Christ. This is the atonement which is the result of the incarnation and the crucifixion. In the incarnation Jesus Christ identified Himself fully with man, assuming human flesh and blood, mind and spirit, becoming a part of the society of man and all its psycho-social relationships. By identification He took up into Himself the whole race of mankind, as He was in them in the sense of His humanity. But Jesus did more than this. He gave Himself for man; that is, in deeds and words of love, forgiveness, and healing, He took their needs upon Himself historically and concretely, pouring out body and soul even unto death for them and their salvation. But still more, He entered into the midst of sinful humanity, assumed this "fallen" humanity, suffered temptation as real as any man's, yet without sin. In this sinful social context He overcame sin. "He became what we are, but did not do what we do."[6]

But it is precisely here that our sinfulness as human beings lies; we not only live in a sinful context and suffer temptation; we are a part of the sinful context and yield to sin. How then can He and we become one body, we sinners one with the sinless One? The distance between us is not just that He is infinite and we are finite, that He is in His resurrected glory and we are earth-bound. The distance between us is the distance of sin, a gap which we of ourselves cannot cross, for we are dead in trespasses and sins; but He crosses the gap by coming to us in reconciliation. This He does on the cross when He accepts God's judgment on us as His own in becoming sin for us, that is, when He accepts the deserved condemnation of the sinner without deserving it Himself. He does this as a participant in the solidarity of the race. We are joined to Him in this by *our* own complete acceptance of our condemnation, and we cannot be joined to Him until we have accepted it, because He has accepted for Himself our condemnation. We die with Him in solidarity.

Christ suffers because of His identification with us sinners and for our sake, and we suffer as we are identified with Him in His suffering for men's sin. Colossians 1:24. He is bound indissolubly with us, and we also with Him, so that "He represents us, stands for us, acts in our behalf, intercedes for us,"[7] and brings us back to God. He lifts us up in Himself as He rises out of the death-condemnation of God; this is our "rising with Him." Thus Christ is representative of and the substitute for the sinner, not in a legalistic and transactional way, but vitally and dynamically, just because He is one with us in our needy and broken, guilty humanity. The incarnation and the atonement are inseparable; the life, death, and resurrection of Christ are inseparable.

Finally, Christ continues to be identified with us men now, intercedes for us, knows our humanity, and will be with us even to the end of the age. He is with us in reality because He is still in solidarity with us men in our humanity, for He did not shed His humanity at the ascension. "The incarnation has a beginning but no ending."[8] The Christ who arose from the dead continues to be one with us in His nature. He still feels our need and gives Himself to us through the Spirit, working out in us the pattern of His humanity, not complete and perfect, indeed, as He was, but working toward this goal. As for us, it is in our humanity, in the context of sinful society, that we must be transformed into His image. He shapes and forms our human manhood, pointing toward the final cleansing and redeeming of our humanity, beyond history, when we shall be like Him.

We have now seen that this vivid figure of the body of Christ is the pictorial representation of God's act in Christ, of Christ's coming to us, giving Himself for us and making possible solidarity with Him, so that we can be one with Him, being incorporated in Him in order that we may receive all that God has to give us through Him. "For in him the whole fulness of deity dwells bodily, and you have come to fulness of life in him" (Colossians 2:9).

But we also have our part in making this union with Christ possible. Just as the response is necessary when God offers to make us His people, so response is necessary to make the body of Christ. The first step is our identification with sinful men in solidarity with the race of the first Adam; this is repentance. The second step is our identification with the historic atoning Christ, in the church's memory of Him as portrayed in the Gospels and the epistles; this is the first part of faith. The third step is our identification now with the Christ of glory, who is with the Father; this is the second part of faith. The fourth step is our response to God in obedience to Christ as Lord; this is the third part of faith. Faith, then, is our total response to God's act in Christ, repenting, believing, trusting, obeying, loving. This decisive act on our part permits the penetration of Christ to the very roots of our selfhood, and because He has laid hold upon us, we "press on to make it . . . [our] own" (Philippians 3:12), "it" including resurrection, life, perfection. God's approach to us in Christ is grace, a grace which is the actual coming of Christ into us, recreating the broken structure of the relationship between us and God in reconciliation. This grace then reconstitutes our existence.[9] The historic Christ becomes part of our past, the central figure in a story which has been made our story. The central decision of our life, to die and be raised, is the decision which Christ in His atonement has already made for us and for all men. It acquires meaning because He has already made it and Himself experienced it, and we enter into it with Him.

The acts of God and Christ described above, together with our response, produce the body of Christ, the church, since our personal central decision of faith identifies us with all other sinners who have made the same decision, and who have thereby been incorporated into Christ. The body of Christ consists of all the redeemed sinners who have been joined to Him in the solidarity of repentance and faith as they have died and risen with Him.

Being now members of the body of Christ, we find ourselves in an interweaving relationship with Him and all other members of the body in whom He also lives, provided all continue to be open to His presence and working as He seeks to work out His purpose in the new humanity of which He is the head. He is available to all because as the ascended one He is freed from all limitations of time and space, limited only by man's openness and response.

Our solidarity with Christ in His body is not basically one of intellect or of feeling, but of will. His will becomes ours. As He always did the will of His Father, so our will becomes to do the will of the Father. This means that the relationship we here speak of is not so much a passive one of status as an active one of function. It produces a mood of joy, but it is the joy not only of reception but also of participation, joy not just of the peace which flows from forgiveness, but also of partnership in a cause. Thus, the entire church as His body becomes the instrument of His operation in the world, the channel of His grace and saving work. The awareness of this calling, and the experience of God's working in us produces ineffable joy.

Our life in this body of Christ is also one of expectation and hope. We know that we still are in need of His working in us in grace to perfect the new humanity in His image, for we as yet share only imperfectly in His nature. We feel the warfare of the two kingdoms in us; we are not always victorious over the old man; we still confess our sins and shortcomings. We long for full cleansing and completion at the Last Day; we not only hope for it but expect it, for Christian hope is not wishing—it is assurance. This does not mean that we deny the presence of Christ in us now. Rather, it is precisely because He is present in us now that we know we have not attained the perfection which is His goal. We continue the struggle with the enemy and accept the suffering which this produces, thus entering into the sufferings of Christ "for the sake of his body" (Colossians 1:24). In doing this we also feel the suffering of the world under its load of sin as Christ felt it. But we also must carry the burden with Christ of seeking to make the church what it ought to be and is intended to be as His body. The church is not now in reality and never has been as a whole the "glorious" body of Christ, blameless and without spot or wrinkle. The perfecting process must go on until the end of time. The presentation of the glorious church occurs at the meeting with the Lord of that church at the end of time.

What we have just outlined, partly from Welch's analysis, is but another way of describing the new birth and the new life in Christ. In conformity to Christ we yield to God's ordering of our life, surrendering our selfish wills, and experiencing concretely the fruit of the Spirit in the new life with its inward and outward progressive transformation of the self into the image of Christ. Romans 8:29; II Corinthians 3:18. In this continuing interaction with Christ and the church each believer accepts covenant responsibility with all his fellows in the body, and all covenant together with the Lord Christ. In another New Testament figure we also become adoptive sons of God, brothers of the Son who is "the first-born among many brethren" (Romans 8:29).

Through this interaction there is a constant stream of influence upon the humanity of the Christian as it is drawn into the being of Christ, so that he can truly say, "I have been crucified with Christ; it is no longer I who live, but Christ who lives in me; and the life I now live in the flesh I live by faith in the Son of God, who loved me and gave himself for me" (Galatians 2:20).

Christ the Head of the Body

The image of Christ as head of the church is closely related to the image of the church as the body of Christ, though not simply a logical derivative of it. The figure appears six times in Ephesians (1:22; 4:15; 5:23) and Colossians (1:18; 2:10; 2:19). Christ's headship of the cosmos—all things—is here directly connected with His headship of the church. Indeed it may be based upon it in the sense that Christ's redeeming work makes Him head of the universe.

Three relationships of the church to Christ are expressed by the metaphor of headship, as the context of Paul's assertions in Ephesians and Colossians shows. (1) The first relationship is that of authority over the church. The church is not autonomous; it is subject to Christ (Ephesians 5:24) as Lord, and is therefore governed by

Him, through the Spirit. The church must hear the voice of her Lord above all other voices; His will must be regnant; His program must be carried through. In this sense the headship of Christ is equivalent to His lordship over the church. Christ expresses Himself through the church as His instrument.

(2) The second relationship expressed by the headship of Christ is that the church finds its goal in Christ, who incorporates in Himself all the purposes of God for the world, and is thus the total ideal toward which the church directs its efforts. It is "to grow up in every way into him who is the head" (Ephesians 4:15), and is to "[hold] fast to the Head, from whom the whole body . . . grows with a growth that is from God" (Colossians 2:19). This metaphor signifies not only that the church sets Christ in His character and person as its distant goal, to be reached eschatologically, but that Christ the Head is working in and with the church now to bring it to His goals. Hence He is said to nourish and cherish it (Ephesians 5:29) and to cleanse and sanctify it with the purpose of presenting it to Himself in ultimate eschatological splendor, as "without spot or wrinkle . . . holy and without blemish" (Ephesians 5:27).

(3) The third implication of the headship relation is that of the unity of the church with Christ in life. The head and body are by nature inseparable, but if the unity is broken by the defection of the body, its life dies.

The Body Image as Expressing the Members' Interrelations

The understanding of the nature of the church which we have now found in the image of the body of Christ up to this point covers only the church's relation to Him. But the relation to Christ also controls the relation of the members of the church to each other. Let us now examine these relations as they exist within the body, for all such relations flow from the common sharing of the life of Christ in His body. The fellowship in the body flows from fellowship with Christ.

The first important aspect of these inner relations of the members is the unity of the body in itself. This should be self-evident, so evident that Paul cries out as he beholds the divisions of the Corinthian church, "Can Christ be divided?" Because we are members of Christ we are members of one another. Romans 12:5. To be in Christ is to be in the church, and to be in the church is to be united in Christ. Neither persons nor groups can be alone in Christ, because all the others who are in Christ are also there. There can be no solitary Christians, as Wesley said. One cannot be in Christ without his brother. The church is not a collection of worshipers who happen to sit side by side in a service, or a group organized to accomplish a task or to perpetuate a tradition, but a body which is integrated into a whole. There are particular vocations of individuals and groups within the body, and there can even be cultivation of various traditions; but this all occurs within the body, not in competition or in contradiction, but in complementation. Paul's insistence in I Corinthians 12 on the Spirit's distribution of gifts to the members and the necessity for their integration into the wholeness of the body by love carries many implications for division of labor, co-operation, and mutuality. Organization is needed of course to carry through in the practice of this mutuality.

It is noteworthy that most of Paul's discussions of the "body of Christ" are found in the context of the discussion of divisions in the church and the need for unity,[10] with the clear import that unity characterizes the body of Christ. The inescapable consequence of this understanding is further that Christ is not found anywhere else on earth but in the church. The church is the realm of redemption.[11] In this sense, the doctrine is true that "outside the church there is no salvation,"[12] provided this is not taken to mean inside only one structured branch of the church. It is in the church that God is saving people; here is where He continues to work in and through them to help work out their salvation in its full meaning.

The unity of the church, of course, does not imply that the personality of the individual member or group is absorbed, overridden, or lost. The church cannot be and do for a member what he must be and do himself. He must as an individual repent and believe, and obey, love, and hope. Yet in all his own experience he knows that the other members of the body have the same experience in Christ, that they are the same sinners saved by grace, and that Christ is in them. Accepting the consequences of this knowledge, he will give and take in the fellowship of the body. He will build up the body and will be built up by it. For this goal he must be in fellowship with the other members, not in schism from them. He must accept them, not cast them off. His full Christian manhood in Christ is experienced only in his self-giving to them. He knows that even in the human sense he is part of all the social texture in which he lives, and that he is not himself apart from the community which has given him so much. Furthermore, he knows that Christ is in all the brethren, seeking to express Himself through them to him as an individual, and that each one has his own gift and ministry through the Spirit. He therefore seeks to open himself to this ministry and receive it to his profit. He becomes a more faithful man thereby and he contributes to the faithfulness of the total body. This theme will be developed more fully in the third chapter, "The Holy Community."

As we compare the actual state of the professing historic and contemporary church with the necessity of unity in the body of Christ, which derives from the fact that it *is* the body of Christ, we face serious problems. Should not the vertical union of each member with Christ express itself in a horizontal unity among the members with each other? Must not the expression of the life of Christ in each be available to others? How dare barriers be erected which block the flow of this life back and forth? Must not unity in theory be expressed in unity in reality?

The answer, of course, to all these questions is Yes. We know that Christ Himself intends it so. John 17 carries this radical call to unity, with the prayer that the disciples may be one as He and the Father are one. John 17:20-22. As stated earlier, in almost every passage where Paul speaks of the body of Christ he uses the figure to overcome disunity. The response to the grace of God in Christ as He offers to us sinners participation in His life must be a response of recognition of our common need and common redemption, and thus of our oneness in Christ.

But what shall we then do in the face of the many historic divisions in the professing church?[13] It is certainly possible to affirm that these divided groups participate, however imperfectly, in the new body created by faith in Christ, and that they accordingly share His grace and life. It is also necessary to confess the sin of division, and to accept the judgment of God upon those who cause divisions and thus destroy the temple of God. I Corinthians 3:17. But does not all this require a further step? Paul's attack on the divisions in Corinth was to overcome them;

confession of sin is to be followed by restitution. The further step, on the one hand, is to take responsibility for sharing with all others what Christ has given us of Himself, and, on the other hand, to open ourselves to Christ's work in all others. Unity by no means implies or requires union in organization or identity in forms or expressions of faith and conduct. There can be and probably ought to be creative diversity so that the witness of Christ in each one and the various gifts of the Spirit in all may have full scope to make their contribution to all. But there should be "no discord in the body, . . . [so] that the members may have the same care for one another" (I Corinthians 12:25). The minimum requirement to make possible this mutual care is that no artificial barriers be created to impede the unity of the Spirit in the bonds of peace, or hinder the ministry of the members to one another. All members of the body of Christ must strive toward that unity of the whole body of Christ which is the will of its Head.

We cannot leave this point, however, without remembering that the real life of the church as a human society is historically and sociologically conditioned. The forms of organization and expression which now operate in the general church, that is, the divided church, have been formed by human action and interaction and become embedded in human tradition, many of them with no malicious purpose or schismatic intent. The constant danger is that we absolutize these human realities. Expressions of the life of the past tend to become so traditional, and thus so hardened and rigid, that they block the flow of life in the body of Christ from member to member and prevent the free action of the Spirit in leading the church in various times and places into creative new action and unity.

Besides unity, common membership in the body of

Christ requires mutual responsibility one for another. The members ought to "have the same care for one another," says Paul. I Corinthians 12:25. They which are spiritual should restore a man overtaken in any trespass. Galatians 6:1. Jesus urges going to the erring brother and seeking to be reconciled with him. Matthew 5:23-25 and 18:15-22. This is a spiritual ministry dictated by love, which should be self-evident, even if it were not so explicitly stated.

The mutual responsibility of the members of the body extends also to material things. Spiritual teachers are to be supported materially by the members who receive the benefit. I Corinthians 9:3-14; Galatians 6:6. Those who have this world's goods should help the needy to food and clothing. James 2:14-17; Romans 12:20; Matthew 25:34-36. In fact, a brother should be ready to lay down his life for the brother. I John 3:16. The concept of the body of Christ is the spiritual foundation for mutual economic aid.

In conclusion, may we note that the fellowship in Christ of which we often speak so familiarly has a much deeper meaning than is often grasped. It is not the easy fellowship of the companionship of friends and acquaintances, or even of the close-knit family. It is the sharing of the common life in the body of Christ.[14] We have fellowship one with another because we share Christ and the Holy Spirit. That is, we have a common possession of Christ and the Spirit; no one member possesses Him alone. And fellowship is intensified by the increasing of each member's share in the common life of the Spirit. This share is inexhaustible, for the Christ who is its life is inexhaustible. The realization of this is what caused Paul to cry out, "Thanks be to God for his inexpressible gift" (II Corinthians 9:15), and to describe his ministry as "to preach . . . the unsearchable riches of Christ" (Ephesians 3:8).

3

THE HOLY COMMUNITY

IT is commonplace today to speak of the church as a fellowship. It is called the fellowship of believers, the fellowship of faith, the fellowship of saints, the fellowship of the Holy Spirit. A closely related term is community; in fact, all of the above designations are used with the word "community" substituted for "fellowship"; for instance, "the community of the Holy Spirit." However, in the New Testament the church is never directly called a fellowship; it has fellowship. Hence, it is probably best to call it a holy community which has fellowship with Christ and whose members have fellowship with each other. But the point to be clearly made is that the church by nature has fellowship; its nature produces community. Unfortunately, all too often both "fellowship" and "community" are used vaguely as a collection of persons in the social sense, without either a clear theological content or praccal meaning. But unless the meanings of these words are given clear and adequate content, the essence of the Biblical meaning of the church as a community having fellowship can be lost. Therefore in this chapter we seek to understand the church as "fellowship community" with the full meaning that the New Testament gives to it.[1]

We start with the basic truth that the experience which makes the church is the common experience of its members. They are all sons of one Father; they all share in an undivided Christ and an undivided Holy Spirit; and they are all members one of another. They are not simply a collection of discrete individuals; they are an organic whole. It is in this sense that the church is an organism and not an organization; it is the result, not of a planned agreement, but of life. Participation in Christ requires participation in one another. Believers in Christ do not decide to have fellowship or to become a community; they are by nature a community. The only question is, Will it be a poor community or a good community, one that remains limited and impoverished or one that achieves its full life? The common life in the body of Christ means both life with Christ in its fullness and a common life together in its fullness. This common life together is the subject of our further consideration.

The most expressive New Testament term for the common life in the body of Christ is the Greek word *koinonia*,[2] which is best translated "fellowship." "Community" is the term to designate the group which has the fellowship. To understand Christian community, however, we must first understand Christian fellowship, for without the latter, community is a purely sociological term, a human construction. The root form *koinonia* in all its derivatives occurs some fifty times in the New Testament, with a common core of meaning, namely, "that which is in common." But varying translations in the King James Version and even in the Revised Standard Version, such as "communication" or "distribution," at times obscure this essential meaning. Modern translations make much use of the word "share" or "sharing," an excellent form to catch the essential meaning, but lacking the personal dimension and warmth that "fellowship" conveys. It is significant to note that approximately half the New Testament occurrences of *koinonia* refer to spiritual sharing, and half to sharing in material goods. This at once lights up the meaning of fellowship.

The root idea in *koinonia* is "participation in something in which others also participate," that is, conscious sharing with someone else in a joint possession, usually on a continuing basis. The German word *Gemeinschaft* conveys this sense well, as does the word *Gemeinde* for church, for the *Gemein-* part of these words means "common."[3] Fellowship is thus much more than mere association or togetherness or any other diluted sense of the term "fellowship," such as having a good time together, although it does involve association. Christian fellowship is to be sharply distinguished from superficial and transient associations. The warm feeling between familiar friends who meet regularly at church meetings, the bonds of an ethnic group with a common language or cultural and historical background, the awareness of a network of related families —all these may have sociological and psychological value in adding to the bonds of loyalty to a common faith which otherwise bind a church membership together, but they cannot carry the life of the Christian community. Group affairs, such as the church supper, the Sunday-school class picnic, the homemakers' club, or the men's brotherhood, may even substitute for Christian fellowship and speed the descent of the church from its high calling in Christ to being merely one of the better social clubs that help to build the community, with religion serving somewhat as background music. A church which has become primarily an ethnic-culture group or a clan of related families, or a community club, is no longer a true church, for it no longer has the New Testament *koinonia* whose life is consciously based on the common possession of Christ and the Spirit. The true Christian community is created and carried by a common body of beliefs, a common life in Christ, and a common commitment to Him in faith and obedience. The quality and strength of this community is directly dependent upon the quality and intensity of this base.

Let us then examine the New Testament concept of *koinonia* to find its full meaning and implications for faith and living.

Koinonia is used twice in the New Testament without any modifying words, although in neither case is it used as a direct name for the church: once in Acts 2:42 ("the fellowship") and once in Galatians 2:9 ("the right hand of fellowship"). In Luke's vivid description of the new people of God immediately following Pentecost, "*the* fellowship" appears as the second of the four marks of the church:[4] "They devoted themselves to the apostles' teaching and [the] fellowship, to the breaking of [the] bread and the prayers" (Acts 2:42). Those who called upon the name of the Lord in repentance and faith and had received the Holy Spirit felt themselves irresistibly drawn apart from all others in Israel into an identifiable close-knit body with such intense and continuous sharing of the mighty acts of God in Christ that they had "the fellowship." No other Jews had what they had—the promise fulfilled, God at work in them, His love poured out upon them, their common mission to witness, their intimate attachment to Christ. They were intensely aware of their belonging together. This spiritual reality also had an immediate effect on their social relationships; they had a common social life.

They spent much time together in the breaking of the bread of the fellowship meals in their homes.

Further, their oneness of heart and soul, says Luke, led to a sharing in material goods, so that "there was not a needy person among them," for "no one said that any of the things which he possessed was his own, but they had everything in common" (Acts 4:32-35; see also Acts 2:44). That is, the particularity of the individual was broken through in every respect, heart and soul and possessions, so that he now participated with the others of the people of God in everything. This was fellowship, not communism.[5] It was love, not economics. This was not a new economic order, although it broke through the conventional limitations of the secular economic order. It was the Christian sense of overwhelming participation in a common life which swept every aspect of life along into it. In contrast, so many Christians since that time, in distressing naiveté, have accepted the prevailing secular economic and social order on its own terms with little or no sense of Christian love and fellowship in this realm. Often the only way that Christian faith operates in it is to produce simple virtues like honesty; Christian love too rarely breaks through the economic order to reorder it. In the apostolic community it did break through. The brother had a claim to the benefit of the temporal possessions of the total community to meet his need, just as he shared in the spiritual possessions of the total community in the grace and power of God in Christ and the Holy Spirit. The apostles' teaching belonged to all; the message of Christ belonged to all; the material needs of each were the concern and responsibility of all. This was Christian love, God's love at work in the community. Their common fellowship meals they therefore called *agape,* this being the

Greek word for divine love in contrast to mere human affection. The church is a community of love—love in action,[6] and love truly exists only in action.

A striking and powerful use of *koinonia* is found in Paul's message to the erring Corinthian church, which was seriously abusing the Lord's Supper. I Corinthians 10 and 11. The King James Version translates *koinonia* here as "communion"; the Revised Standard Version makes it "participation." "The cup of blessing which we bless, is it not a *koinonia* in the blood of Christ? The bread which we break, is it not a *koinonia* in the body of Christ? Because there is one loaf, we who are many are one body, for we all partake of the same loaf" (I Corinthians 10:16, 17). Here the communion service is not just a memorial of Christ's death; it is a visible act of testimony to a common fellowship in the body. The sin of the Corinthian abuse of the Supper, for which Paul charged them with eating and drinking unworthily, was the sin of the breach of fellowship in the church on class lines, right at the communion table, which implied a similar breach in the life of the church as a whole. The body of Christ was thereby not "discerned"; that is, the true meaning of fellowship in the body of Christ was missed, for to claim participation in His body while breaking brotherly fellowship with fellow members in the church was to deny the reality of the body of Christ. He who does this heaps judgment upon himself, for in effect he destroys the *koinonia.*

The meaning of Paul's rebuke is that the sin of pride and selfishness is a denial of Christ's body and requires the exclusion from the Supper of those who are guilty of this sin. Here is the true ground and necessity for close communion—fellowship with Christ in the Supper means fellowship with the persons who partake of the Supper.

Those who violate the body of Christ in act cannot partake of the body of Christ symbolically. To eat the bread and drink the cup is a declaration that one lives by feeding on Christ, that Christ's life is the basis for one's living, that one is therefore committed to follow Him, that one is a member of His body. Only those can honestly partake of the Supper who mean this. If the Supper is merely for the private edification of individuals worshiping Christ by remembering His dying grace and love, then, to be sure, close communion has no meaning or justification. But if it represents a common life and common discipleship, that life must be expressed both in the symbol and in the act. Since it is the church as the body of Christ that determines the nature of the discipleship, the church must determine the boundaries of the communion table. So one's theology of the Supper and his understanding of the meaning of fellowship in the body of Christ will determine his position on close communion.

It is thus apparent that *koinonia* is of the very essence of the church, which draws its common life from God the Father, Christ the Son, and the Holy Spirit. Sharing this love which has redeemed us and keeps us in His grace makes us inevitably one in heart, soul, and spirit, and results in mutual love among the members. *Koinonia* therefore always carries the dual reference, the divine and the human, for the *koinonia* which pertains to human fellowship always points beyond itself to its source. The character and significance of the human fellowship is drawn from its relationship to God in and through Christ.

But the important thing to note is that the human fellowship, *koinonia,* is essential to the church. The individual who has been redeemed by grace will be drawn into true community with the other human persons in the church and thus express the *koinonia* in concrete human relations. *Koinonia* is no abstract theological principle nor poetic speculation; it is the fact of experience for multitudes of Christians from apostolic times to the present in their human life. It ought to be the experience of all Christians.

It is therefore important to understand the church as a human community, for the often-heard declaration, "The church is divine, not human," is patently not a Scriptural notion. Even the statement, "The church is an organism, not an organization," quoted above, can be, as we shall see, a serious overstatement.

An essential requirement for the functioning of the human community whether in limited local congregations, general organizations, institutions, agencies, or representative or delegated bodies of any kind is that there be communication among the members. Practically, fellowship comes to a concrete focus when Christians actually meet together, and a regular sharing of a common life is necessary for its full development. The local congregation of believers is the best expression of this full fellowship. But wherever there is communication even across considerable distances, where there can be knowledge of a common faith, testimony to a common experience, awareness of spiritual concerns, sharing of blessings and needs, participation in joint action, there is fellowship and community, even if the warmth and intensity of face-to-face contact is missing. Christian fellowship is not limited to the sociological primary group, but if the local congregation is too large for the fullest fellowship the congregation will be able to fulfill only partially and in weakness a major reason for its existence. It should then either be broken up organizationally into smaller congregations where a fuller fellowship can be exercised, or it should form smaller fellowship groups within itself for this purpose.[7] Having made clear that Christian fellowship can function at all levels and in all structures it still remains to be said that the smaller local fellowship group is the primary carrying ground for the life of the church.

In the light of our definition of fellowship it is clear that the basic experience of fellowship, as well as its growth in meaning and intensity, is dependent upon the awareness of a common experience of the grace of God in Christ, a common response of faith and obedience, a common expression of Christian love. This awareness must be communicated interpersonally by the witness of the members to each other of their common experience and by mutual admonition to Christian obedience and action, and must be heightened by an ever-deepening understanding and appreciation of the grace of God as it works in the fellowship. The members of the body of Christ will be in submission to each other and will take binding action for each other, for ethical decision will be made in the context of the church where Christ is the head. This does not mean that all the decisions of life for the individual must be turned over to the local congregation for disposal. Rather, it means that the basic standards for governing life will be established by the church and will have binding force on the individuals. These group standards then become guides for the individual, pointing out to him the right way of conduct and service, making his duties and obligations clear, warning him of sin. To refuse "to hear the church" is to deny the nature of the church; "Let him be unto thee as an heathen man and a publican" (Matthew 18:17, KJV).

In fulfilling its fellowship the whole community will

bear the burdens of all both spiritually and materially. There will not only be mutual discipline as Jesus outlines it in Matthew 18 and as Paul does in I Corinthians 5, but mutual aid, as enjoined by Paul in Galatians 6 and as illustrated in the collection for the saints in Jerusalem in II Corinthians 8 and 9. There will be "fellowship in the gospel," that is, a sharing in the proclamation of the Gospel in evangelism. The whole apparatus of Christian action, in evangelism, Christian education, mutual aid, social service, if it is to include all the members of the body of Christ, however widely distributed over a broad geographical area or in various countries, does, of course, require organization and structure, and channels of communication. But this structure must be based on the fundamental fellowship in Christ and with one another if it is to be truly an expression of the nature of the church and really Christian. Conversely, if the fellowship really exists, it must express itself in joint action and common experience; it is not just a feeling the members have for each other, a vague sense of belonging together, a species of human friendship, or a theological declaration.

Another way to express the meaning of the *koinonia* is to use the term "brotherhood" for the church, and "brethren" for its members. This image of the church as a brotherhood is taken from the concept of Christians as the children of God, members of a common family with one Father, of Christ as the "firstborn among many brethren" (Romans 8:29, also Hebrews 2:11) and of all the disciples as brothers to one another. The term "brethren" is the most frequent designation of Christians in the New Testament, being used some 250 times in this way in Acts and the epistles, 130 times by Paul alone, 50 times in Acts, 35 times just in I Corinthians. Peter calls the church "the brotherhood" when he says, "Love the brotherhood" (I Peter 2:17). Brotherhood means mutual love and responsibility, full participation of all in the family of God, full sharing in the ordering of the life of the church, in exactly the same sense as fellowship does. It means a love because of which all the members minister to each other in all their needs, both temporal and spiritual. The church is a brotherhood in which there are no ranks or levels of distinction in honor or superiority. There are distinctions of gifts and duties, but not of superiority and inferiority. There is not a class of clergy and a class of laity. "Neither be called masters," said Jesus, "for you have one master, the Christ," "and you are all brethren" (Matthew 23:10, 8).

The basic understanding of the nature of the church at which we have arrived in our examination of the concept of fellowship and community must also find expression in the structure of the church and in the ordering of its life, government, and discipline. All the members of the body, if they are to fulfill their function, must carry concern and responsibility for the ordering of the life of the church, and all must have the possibility of expressing this responsibility.

Two dangers threaten the full development of the potential of fellowship and brotherhood and its right expression in the life of the church. The one is individualism, the other, institutionalism. Individualism is the overgrowth and perversion of the sense of personal responsibility and importance which results in withdrawal from the common life, going one's own way, refusal to receive the admonition and counsel of the brother or the brotherhood, insistence upon one's own rightness, disinclination to sharing. In its full growth such individualism breaks the bonds of the common life. It turns the rightful and needed sense of individual responsibility before God, and the need for a personal experience of Christ and the Holy Spirit, into the corrupted spirit of self-exaltation.

On the other hand, the development of a faulty church polity and organizational structure which excludes the individual from sharing responsibility in the common life and relegates the direction and ordering of the affairs of the church to a few, whether in the local congregation or in the larger relationships of the church, is bound to have the effect not only of encouraging the passivity of the individual but of a loss of interest in and sense of responsibility for the welfare of the brother and of the church as a whole. The result is a breakdown in fellowship and a denial of the very nature of the church.

This is not to deny the need for representative organization and structure if there is to be any real participation of local elements in the larger life of the church, or a division of labor if there is to be co-operation, or the need for institutions for specialized functions. It is only to say that the structure must be so planned and the organization and institution so operated that the total membership is involved and can give and receive counsel in all things, directly or indirectly. Responsibility requires involvement, and involvement requires channels. Leadership is essential, but it must operate in such a way as to maintain the participation of the total brotherhood in the total life of the church. The starting point for this is a vital and warm spiritual fellowship and participation in the local brotherhood.

The principle of membership participation in the ordering of the life of the church extends to nurture and discipline. The spiritual welfare of each individual must be the concern of all. If the life of Christ in the membership is to flow through open channels from one to the other, there must be the possibility not only of mutual communication but also of enlistment of spiritual concern. The restoration of the erring brother must be an expression of the love and spiritual strength of all. The concrete measures of nurture and discipline should be the expression of the will of all, even though this expression may need to be through delegated action by individuals, and even though there will certainly be numerous cases of personal and pastoral counseling and confession and restitution that will be handled in private and not dealt with in public. Effective church discipline in the restorative, not the punitive, sense cannot be operated except in the context of the redemptive community of believers. And this redemptive attitude will require that all the members act and speak in love and not in judgment, condemnation, and rejection. To make only one person, even the pastor, carry both decision and execution, with the possible inference that the membership does not share in it, can seriously vitiate or even block the spiritual healing and helping effect of the love of the brotherhood.

Ultimately discipline may also involve exclusion from the fellowship, but this can have little meaning except within the framework of a high concept of the nature of that fellowship. This high concept means a fellowship not only in receiving the redeeming grace of God, but also in responding to this grace in obedience. It is not only a fellowship of "saved sinners" but a fellowship of saints striving after holiness. It is not only the called body of Christ, but also the bride which Christ is seeking "to purify for himself a people of his own who are zealous for good deeds" (Titus 2:14), which He loves and nourishes "that he might sanctify her . . . , that she might be holy and without blemish" (Ephesians 5:26, 27). This sanctifying, nourishing, purifying striving after holiness proceeds within the context of the body, within the dynamics of the fellowship. To be in the church is to be in that sphere where Christ lives, where He is Lord, and where the Spirit of God operates and there is dynamic striving after holiness. To be out of the church is to be denied any relationship to Christ and the Spirit and to be in the realm of the devil's dominion. To withdraw the fellowship of the church from a member is therefore to do a most serious thing; it means, as Paul says in I Corinthians 5:5 (see also I Timothy 1:20), to deliver someone to Satan, to exclude him from the place where Christ is recognized as Lord and the Holy Spirit operates in power. Here are Paul's exact words, which seem at first sight to be harsh and unloving: "When you are assembled . . . with the power of our Lord Jesus, you are to deliver this man to Satan for the destruction of the flesh [that is, the fleshly principle in him], that his spirit may be saved in the day of the Lord Jesus." The decline or absence of discipline in a church, combined with the absence of real *koinonia,* makes this statement not only incomprehensible but intolerable. Yet we cannot minimize the seriousness of exclusion from the fellowship of the body of Christ. Newbigin states it thus:

> When Paul writes to the Corinthians about the excommunication of the erring brother, it is very clear that he does *not* say nor imply that it is simply a matter of the sinner cutting himself off. He calls for a very solemn and deliberate act of the fellowship—an act in which he himself is completely associated. Moreover this act is not regarded as merely a severance of external membership while leaving the man's spiritual relationship with Christ untouched. It is a matter of the most awful spiritual meaning—nothing less than delivering him to Satan. Surely

> we have to face the fact that, whatever we may make of it, Paul and his converts were alike working with a conception of the church which made membership in it a tremendous spiritual reality. To be in its fellowship was to be in Christ, and to be cast out of it was to be delivered over to Satan.[8]

It must be said again, however, that such ultimate exclusion from the fellowship has little meaning or force if membership in the fellowship itself has little meaning or effect. If, however, life-giving power and healing has been experienced in the brotherhood, if love and forgiveness, spiritual counsel and restoration have been real, then the withdrawal of these realities has the possibility of genuine influence. It goes without saying, of course, that such ultimate discipline is only for the impenitent sinner for whom all restorative measures have proved ineffective, who resists the Holy Spirit as He operates in the fellowship, and consequently prevents the ministry of the brotherhood from reaching him.

The depth of meaning and potential in the Christian fellowship, then, requires that the church find all possible channels and means for this life of fellowship to come to expression. It cannot remain only an inner spiritual ideal but must be expressed in the real, visible life of the human beings who constitute the church. It is the responsibility of the leadership along with the members to see that channels are opened for this expression. The Holy Spirit dwells in the church, which is, as Paul declares, the habitation of God in the Spirit. But this dwelling is in the human persons who constitute the church; in other words, the church is the habitation of the Spirit in the flesh. His work in the church is dependent upon human instrumentation and channels. Since He works in the church as a body, there must be interpersonal channels and structures of relationship. Should these channels be nonexistent, choked, or cut off, His work stops. It is the human community which is the carrier of the work of the Holy Spirit, and the Spirit cannot work if the community does not exist.

If we then see the church, the total church or any part of it, as a human community, we must ask whether the relationship which this community bears to Christ in any way suspends the common social processes that operate in all human communities and relationships—or indeed, whether the human fallibilities of ordinary mortals are eliminated in the church, whether sin is eradicated, whether the flesh ceases to function within the church. To ask the question is to have the answer, for the picture of the church in the New Testament, from Ananias to Demas and the Nicolaitans from Jerusalem and Corinth to Laodicea, belies any such concept. The warnings against the sins of the flesh and the sins of the spirit, whether given by Paul, Peter, James, or John, forbid any notion of a divine perfection for the church on this side of the end of history. And even if the New Testament did not settle the question for us, the two-thousand-year history of the church furnishes more than sufficient evidence. In all this we do not deny in any sense the operation of grace in this very human church, grace for overcoming, and power for victory. The long history of the church furnishes much evidence for this also.

Why emphasize the humanity of the church and its chronic weakness? Because there seems often to be among Christians, as we speak of the church, a serious distortion of perspective which so idealizes the church as to make it unrecognizable historically. As a consequence, our discourse becomes ethereal, or mystical, without relevance to actual human Christians, and the concept of the invisible church tends to come in in an attempt to save the ideal of the church. This may be a real theological distortion which is genuinely unscriptural, as any monergism which denies the freedom and responsibility of the human will, or any interpretation of the Christian life which reduces man to passivity, or any doctrine of absolute perfection. In our humanity, as in the incarnation of Christ, the divine does not suspend the human but works through it. It is in this sense, too, that the church's life compares to that of her incarnate Lord. Any minimizing of the real humanity of Jesus calls the atonement into question, and threatens His saving work. Any minimizing of the humanness of the church threatens its functioning on the earth. The laws of the social process—psychology and sociology—still operate in the human relations of Christians.

The recognition of the humanness of the church carries with it the recognition of the inevitability, indeed need, of human institutions. Human life must have forms. The life is not in the forms, but creates and controls the forms. The essence of the church is not institutional; it does not exist to maintain institutions; but its humanness requires and takes on institutional forms. An illustration of this is that if there is to be united and common action, there must be structure and channels.

The church then is inevitably an institution, granting its humanness, though not only an institution. Its forms of action and relationship necessarily become routinized, accepted, embedded in culture and the social process. Just as inevitably as any institution it bears the marks of the culture in which it exists and operates. In fact, it must do this to be relevant to its environment. As institutional forms are accepted in the activity of the church, general or local, however, they must be made to serve the church's purpose without compromising her essential nature and mission. It is the church's obligation to protect itself from the debilitation and corruption which institutionalization can bring.

Institutions are necessary not only because of the humanness of the church, but also because of the church's work and expansion in the world. If the sole obligation of the church were to gather for praise and worship and to rejoice in God's mercies, perhaps it could get along without much institutionalization. But it has much work to do, and a great commission to fulfill. Jesus Himself created the apostolic twelve as an institution with authority which the church recognized. The Jerusalem church had a relief committee of seven with an organized soup kitchen financed by the apostolic treasurer's office. To solve a problem of relationship between the Jerusalem and Judean church and the Gentile churches in Syria and Cilicia, a general conference was called, composed of Antiochian delegates, the apostles, and the board of elders of the Jerusalem church. This representative body worked out the solution, with James in charge as moderator. The function of the whole church in Jerusalem was only to ratify the decision reached by the counseling body, that is, by the apostles, elders, and delegates from Antioch. Paul structured an organization of district superintendents for at least part of his field, giving supervisory duties to Timothy and Titus. The elder of III John was probably a traveling supervisor.[9] There were bishops or elders in the early church, though apparently no formal preaching office as such. These were in effect institutionalized offices.

Institutions, representative or nonrepresentative, are humanly necessary for any co-operation beyond local meeting groups or for any division of labor. Through the ordination of representative leaders, through delegated conferences, through boards and committees, through local specialized institutions the church becomes institutionalized. There is nothing wrong or unscriptural about this, and the only alternative to it is the collapse of any real co-operation or division of labor, or a rampant individualism with self-appointed leaders, self-appointed operators, self-appointed authorities.

The record of church history shows that institutions can get in the way of the Spirit, that clerical authorities can become authoritarian, that trust can be placed in buildings, liturgies, music, and money, that boards, committees, and agencies and their executive officials may rule instead of serving. Education can become a cure-all, and trust in material things can become more powerful than trust in God. The general structure of the church can make it difficult for the local voice to be heard, and result in a general suppression of participation of the members in the life of the church. A professional pastor can help to turn the congregation into a nonparticipating audience, and a traditional authoritarian lay minister, who makes all the decisions himself, can also reduce the congregation to silence.

But there are also grave dangers in the opposite direction. Small groups can ignore the counsel of the whole church. Aggressive individuals can dominate congregations. Highly individualized persons or groups can become unwilling to "submit themselves" to one another in the total church, can frustrate the work of the church, can break fellowship, destroy co-operation, cause schism, and inhibit the Spirit's working. In both extremes the worst can happen. But it need not happen. The dangers can be seen and overcome, if not at once, yet in time with patience and love. The failure of some institutions is no argument against the institutional principle. The overruling consideration is that the general church is the body of Christ—not a few persons or only local congregations. Sound church life and structure must make possible the co-operation and mutuality of the entire church, and the enlistment of all its resources. They must make possible hearing the Spirit as He speaks through all the members. The general church dare not be atomized by a false congregationalism. While we may not be able to structure fully the whole of the general church, it must at least go as far as the boundaries of the denominational brotherhood of which the local congregations are parts.

This is the picture of the human sociological church, composed of persons living in their humanity, subject to all the normal social processes of any human society, needing the help of good organization, sound methods, and effective leadership. This same church is at the same time also the community of the common life in the body of Christ, the community of believers, disciples, and saints, the community of love in which Christ is Lord through the Spirit.

In the concluding portion of this chapter, let us consider the church as the community of the Holy Spirit, in the sense that the church is the sphere in which the Holy Spirit operates. We shall here not consider the entire doctrine of the Holy Spirit, but limit our examination to His relation to the church. There is a refreshing and heartening revival of interest and concern in this field, and much new understanding is being brought to light from the current study of the New Testament and contemporary theological endeavor. At the same time, there is considerable confusion, owing in part to the fact that the teaching on the Holy Spirit is not simple and clear and not readily systematized.

"The Bible does not attempt a detailed definition of who the Spirit is; rather, on page after page, it tells us what the Spirit does. He operates with 'overwhelming, revolutionary, transforming results,' declares theologian Emil Brunner. He works through the imperfect, through earthen vessels, so we never see Him as He is, but we know Him in His work in and through men."[10]

Luke's account of the descent of the Spirit at Pentecost is one illustration of this Biblical reporting. Something unforgettable and of unique import happened at Pentecost, something powerful enough to redirect the course of history and to change the quality of millions of lives. After the barriers between God and rebellious men had been removed by Calvary and the resurrection, the Spirit could be shed on the church as He had never operated among men before. And after Pentecost "the early church recognized its great dependence upon the Spirit; it attributed its successful preaching, its conversions, its healings, and its very continuation under strife to the work of the Spirit."[11] Although no explanation is given as to the mode of the Spirit's operation, it is clear that His work is central in the life of the church. "The church exists not by its structure and form, but by the Holy Spirit," as Donald Miller says.[12] The outpouring of the Holy Spirit and the very existence of the church are directly connected. As Newbigin says, "the church is, in the most exact sense, a *koinonia,* a common sharing of the Holy Spirit."[13] It is the work of the Spirit to create, deepen, and extend the *koinonia* in the church. The Spirit is the means by which Christ and the church are united in one body. It is the Spirit which makes us His, for "any one who does not have the Spirit of Christ does not belong to him" (Romans 8:9), and "no one can say 'Jesus is Lord' except by the Holy Spirit" (I Corinthians 12:3). The Spirit produced the New Testament Scriptures by the inspiration of the apostles and their associates, and He guides the church to the Scriptures and in the use of them. He empowers the church for witness and service.

Any consideration of the relation of the Spirit to the church must start with the recognition of the inseparable union between Christ and the Spirit. This implies at once the inseparability of the body of Christ and the Spirit. As Christ identifies Himself in gracious self-giving with the church as His body, so the Spirit identifies Himself with the church. The New Testament calls this a dwelling of the Spirit in the church. I Cor. 3:16; Eph. 3:22. God imparts the Spirit to the church, and this means to the entire body, not just to certain very "spiritual" members. The Spirit and the church are inseparable. He is the corporate possession of the church in which all members participate in common. Since Pentecost there has been no Christian without the Spirit; all members of the church have the Spirit and need not ask for Him. He is not a quantity of which one can have more or less, but a Person with whom one has fellowship. The only question is, How truly and fully does the Christian or the church respond to the Spirit's work? "To be filled with the Spirit" is merely a figurative way of saying that full entrance has been granted to the Spirit to work His way in all things in the life of the believer and in the life of the church. Nor need His departure be feared, for He will abide with us forever. John 14:16. The important thing is that the Spirit is always present in the whole church and every member of it, in every subdivision, agency, organization, and institution, seeking to work His will, even though He is not always properly recognized, nor always listened to. It is not true that only individuals have the Spirit, and that they have Him only when they are acting as individuals. He is as fully present in representative bodies as in the local congregation, in a working agency as in a single person, in a board or committee as in the "two or three . . . gathered together." In fact, He has greater scope for effectiveness in a group than in an individual. In the New Testament in almost every case of the Spirit's bestowal He was given to groups, to the whole company of disciples, to families. He was seldom given to individuals alone.

The thrust of these observations is to make it clear that essentially the Holy Spirit operates within the church and for the benefit and blessing of the church. H. Wheeler Robinson's declaration is right when he says that the "gifts of the Spirit are bestowed on the community, in the community, and for the community, and the spirit of selfish display or ostentatious individualism comes from another quarter."[14] The Spirit *usually* chooses to work through the church as a body and not through individuals separately. He *normally* pleases to work through the *koinonia.* He is not confined to the organized church, however, and history contains more than one example of God's raising up prophets and reformers to recall the church to lost truth and forsaken ways of righteousness, when renewal came through courageous minorities or dedicated individuals of unusual spiritual discernment and power when the official channels of the church's life were clogged or leaders had become corrupt or selfish. An individual may at times be led of the Spirit to stand against his fellow members in witness or warning. But this must always be in the interest of the whole brotherhood, never for personal power or prestige, and must first and last be a loving witness to the brotherhood, not an attack on it. It must take place inside the church, not as a schismatic operation.

We have seen that Spirit and church may not be set against each other. Likewise, the Spirit may not be set over against the Word. Christ meets us in the Scriptures, and it is in these Scriptures that the Holy Spirit makes the truth of Christ alive, so that it bears fruit. Since it is the same Holy Spirit who inspired the Scriptures who moves in our hearts today, men who move in directions contrary to the Scriptures cannot claim the guidance of the Spirit. We assert then further that Word and Spirit together become the authority above and over the church and its traditions. This understanding does not ignore in favor of the letter of Scripture the living Spirit of Christ which is present in the church. On the contrary the church with right may claim the guidance of Him as its head, but this guidance must be confirmed and controlled by appeal to the Scriptures, and in particular to the New Testament. The Scriptures, of course, are not to be understood in a wooden manner, but dynamically, and must be subject to intelligent interpretation and application in the light of current needs. However, any appeal to an inner light above and beyond the Scriptures, even though it be called the light of the Holy Spirit or the Spirit of Christ, is properly suspect. Christ, the Holy Spirit, and the Word are one in a dynamic union; they may not be separated without the risk of grievous loss.

On the other hand, the church is always in danger of resisting the Holy Spirit. And who of us can claim he has never resisted, never grieved, never quenched the Holy Spirit? The gravest dangers here are two: (1) that the traditions of the past may stifle the voice of the Spirit today;

or (2) that leaders may seek to hold power in their own hands, and resist the Spirit moving in others in the church. In either case, the result is the same. Where God would lead forward and upward, or would cleanse and purge, men resist. They resist opening themselves to new light; they refuse to respond to calls for new work; they resist change; hallowed traditions are given unwarranted religious sanction or even presumed Scriptural endorsement; culture is confused with faith; commandments of men are made into commandments of God; institutions and administrators reject legitimate criticism, the brotherly address. So the Spirit is stifled, His will is thwarted, the true nature of the fellowship is broken, and life is finally turned into that death when men no longer will hear what the Spirit says to the churches.

Let our prayer for the church therefore be that of the Pauline triune benediction: "The grace of the Lord Jesus Christ and the love of God and the fellowship of the Holy Spirit be with you all" (II Corinthians 11:14).

4

BELIEVERS, DISCIPLES, AND SAINTS

THE three terms in the title of this chapter all speak of the response of the members of the church to its Redeemer and Lord. Except for the term "brother," with their verb and adjective cognates they are the most frequently used designations for Christians in the New Testament, each appearing several hundred times. It is important to note that almost all the New Testament designations for the members of the church, not only these three names listed above, are descriptive terms which conceive of the members as responding to Christ rather than only or primarily as receiving from Him. As characteristics they become in a real sense requirements for membership in the church. Without them men cannot really be Christians, and the church does not come into being. The response always follows God's approach, to be sure; His call and promise are prior to the response. His acts furnish the basis for the response; His grace makes possible the response; His Spirit and grace work in and with the responding people to produce the response. It is in the context of all that God has done and still is doing for all the members of the church that the individual responds. But the response is nevertheless that of responsible persons whose will is engaged and who must be active in the response. In this picture of the church, God's side and man's side cannot be separated. Man's side must not be overlooked; to deny it is to deny the church's humanity. Paul combines the two perfectly in his joyous exclamation: "I can do all things through Christ which strengtheneth me" (Philippians 4:13, KJV).

Let us now examine the meaning of each of these three concepts—believers, disciples, saints—to find what each contributes to the composite picture of what the responding church should be.

Believers

The overwhelming evidence of the New Testament is that on the human side faith is the constitutive element in the establishment of the church as God's people. As we have seen in the first chapter, it was also constitutive for membership in the people of God under the old covenant. In both covenants it is the response to the grace of God in full commitment to Him. The true and only people of God in all ages is the people of faith, but it is in the new covenant that this is sharply and definitively said. Peter laid down the terms of entrance into the new community of Christ's people at Pentecost in radical terms: "Repent, and be baptized every one of you in the name of Jesus Christ for the forgiveness of your sins; and you shall receive the gift of the Holy Spirit" (Acts 2:38). And when at the Jerusalem Council twenty years later he recalled this Pentecostal moment, he said: "Brethren, you know that in the early days God made choice among you, that by my mouth the Gentiles should hear the word of the gospel and believe" (Acts 15:7).[1]

Before Peter, Jesus had already stated in identical terms the requirements for entrance into the kingdom, in His initial proclamation at the beginning of His public ministry: "Repent, and believe in the gospel" (Mark 1:15). And when He was asked, "What must we do, to be doing the work of God?" He replied: "This is the work of God, that you believe in him whom he has sent" (John 6:28, 29). And again He declared, "Truly, truly, I say to you, he who believes has eternal life" (John 6:47). John 3:16 says, "Whoever believes in him should not perish but have eternal life." The apostles' reply to the Philippian jailer may be taken as a summary of all the apostolic answers to inquirers: "Believe in the Lord Jesus, and you will be saved" (Acts 16:31). The church cannot be understood, either in its origin or in its continuance, except as a fellowship of believers. It is the community of faith.

We stand at a crucial point in our doctrine of the church. Is the church a body of believers only (however weak or inadequate the faith may be), or does it incorporate those who do not and cannot have a living faith and experience of their own? If it is the former, the church is composed of voluntary, committed, and obedient disciples, a disciplined church, striving to know and to do the will of its Lord in fullness. This, we hold, is the New Testament ideal. The second position posits the inclusivist church of all the people, the *Volkskirche,* the traditional church. The incorporation of infants who cannot know or consent to membership, and the retention of all members regardless of the maintenance of faith and life are both consequences and causes of the deterioration of the church from a fellowship of faith to an indifferent population Christianized by definition. Culture is then baptized along with the population, the distinction between church and world is wiped out, and the church becomes a religious institution, mediating salvation by a priesthood or a clergy, or administering grace by an apparatus of pastors and theologians. That there unquestionably are true believers in such a church does not make it a true church of Christ, for it is an impossible mixture of believers and unbelievers. It is one of the incredible paradoxes of history that the Reformers, who so boldly and effectively recaptured the Gospel of grace from its medieval distortion and restored the central message of justification by faith, should have retained the mass church of the mixed multitude, the territorial church of the Constantinian compromise, in which real faith was not a requirement for membership. The attempts of a Luther to close the unbridgeable gap between his concept of salvation by faith and his concept of the mass church by various constructs such as a proxy faith of godparents for baptized infants, or a divinely inserted faith, only serve to indicate the impossibility of the undertaking. The necessity of turning baptism into a sacramental regeneration to accomplish this purpose is another evidence of the difficulty resulting from the wrong concept of faith.[2]

We have arrived at the point where we must examine the way in which an unbeliever is brought to that faith which alone makes possible his incorporation into the fellowship of believers. In other words, how does a man get into the church of believers? Here we must answer the question, What does it mean to believe in the Lord Jesus Christ? And since in the New Testament baptism is the act of initiation into the visible church, we shall find some of the clearest teaching on the meaning of saving faith in passages which combine the symbolism of baptism with direct teaching on this subject.

The classic source for the teaching on the meaning of saving faith is Romans 1–8, climaxed in chapter 6, verses 1-14, seconded by Colossians 2:6-15 and 3:1-11, and Galatians 2:20, 21 and 6:14-16. The theme of Romans is a right relationship with God by faith in Christ. In chapter 4 Paul shows that a right relationship never existed through works and ceremonies, for if one goes back far enough he finds that Abraham's acceptance was by faith. Chapter 5 shows that faith in Christ is central for access to God's reconciliation with man through Christ, proving that salvation does not come by obedience to a code of precepts. The universal dominion of sin that has come over men has been replaced by a reign of grace for all who will unite with Christ by faith. Paul sums up by saying, "Where sin increased, grace abounded all the more" (Romans 5:20). Realizing at once, however, the danger that this teaching of more abounding grace might result in a misunderstanding of the nature of salvation, Paul poses the question whether the believer should seek to get more grace by more sinning, and in the process of answering it gives the most profound and dynamic understanding of the meaning of faith, grace, and salvation to be found anywhere in the New Testament. In so doing he penetrates radically to the very heart of the Christian experience of faith.

Here is Paul's line of thought in Romans 6:1-14. It is completely unreasonable to expect anyone who has real faith in Christ to continue in sin. Why? Because the life of the believer is transformed by his union with Christ through faith in the following way: Christ's work for our salvation is His dying by crucifixion and coming to new life by resurrection. When He died, He broke all connection with the sinful world which crucified Him, and by

His resurrection proved His defeat of the enemy and His full capacity to continue to triumph over all that the enemy could do, including death, and to accomplish throughout the coming ages the redemption of men. In this He identified His will completely with the will of God. The believer then by faith identifies himself with the acts of Christ. He submits his will to God's will; he dies in that he spiritually breaks all connection with the old environment and power of sin, and is raised by God's grace to newness of life in a spiritual resurrection. The believer's identification of himself with Christ is described by the Greek word *sumphutoi* (Romans 6:5), which literally means "grown together."[3] Here is the crucial point. The believer must identify his will with Christ's as grown together with His in complete renunciation of the dominion of sin.

Hence, the baptismal question is fully in order, "Are you truly sorry for your past sins, and are you willing to renounce Satan, the world, and all works of darkness and your own carnal will and sinful desires?"[3a] To commit oneself thus is to be "crucified with Christ" or "dying with him," in Paul's powerful phrases. Such identification with Christ is a conscious voluntary act of faith committing the entire personality. This is believing "*in* Christ" (the Greek original often has "*into* Christ"), as the Revised Standard Version has it; and the Revised Standard Version substitution of believing *in* Christ for believing *on* Christ is a real advance in clarifying the meaning of believing. "Believing *on*" to modern ears carries the connotation of intellectual assent, that is, believing something to be true, whereas "believing *in*" or "into" is a movement of the will that identifies one with Christ or God in vital commitment to a person. This radical break with the past, the breaking off of all former allegiances, is the result of the Spirit's operation. It is a regeneration, a new birth. But it is made possible by the movement of the human will. Again, we see the inseparable relationship of God's action in free grace through Christ to man's free response. The heart of the Christian experience of conversion is thus simply the ultimate application of the central truth we have seen thus far in all the relations of God to man in redemption, whether figured in the image of the people of God, or the body of Christ, or the community of the Holy Spirit. God acts and man responds.

To summarize: Belief in the Lord Jesus Christ is not something essentially forensic, theological, or ethical; it is personal commitment and identification which places one "in Christ," that is, in the sphere of His operation, so that one can thereby live victoriously over sin. T. C. Smith says it thus: "One does not become triumphant himself merely by participating in the triumph [of Christ]. He becomes triumphant only as his own life relives that which Christ did."[4]

In this personal and dynamic experience of the renewed human will there comes the central point of realizing actual possession of that which is offered in Christ, the free gift of grace which is the intention of Christ for us and which was beforehand made possible by His death and resurrection. This sense of possession is co-ordinated with the inward knowledge that we *have* responded. This is the "assurance of faith," that is, the assurance produced by faith. This is true conversion. We receive the benefits of the victory which Christ has achieved.

To be sure, the meaning of the breach with the dominion of sin as well as the acceptance of the reign of grace, that is, the lordship of Christ, must still be worked out in full content. To this Paul admonishes in the following verses in Romans 6, as well as in Colossians 3. There is to be the "killing" (mortifying) of single sins as they become clear to the conscience; there is to be the "[yielding of] yourselves to God as men who have been brought from death to life, and your members to God as instruments of righteousness" (Romans 6:13); there is to be a yielding step by step to all known calls to ethical behavior and service. This is enlarging the scope of the victory which was basically won in the dying and rising which is the starting point of the new life. Now that the will is captive to Christ, His will must be worked out in all the meanings of life to come. The dying and rising is the death to self which Christ requires of all those who would be His disciples, with its sequel of daily cross-bearing and following Christ. Discipleship follows this death. As Bonhoeffer has strikingly stated it, "When Christ calls a man, He bids him come and die."[5]

Before taking up discipleship, however, a word must be said about baptism. Romans 6 and the passages cited in Galatians and Colossians are not discussions of baptism. The topic of baptism is only incidental to the discussion of faith and new life. But the inference is legitimate that faith and new life were required for baptism. External water baptism is a declaration of the church, in agreement with the believer, that the experience described in Romans 6 has actually occurred. The candidate for baptism must therefore be capable of making the required commitment to Christ and must openly confess that this has happened. As a rite of initiation, baptism matches the union with Christ by incorporation into the visible fellowship of believers.

On this understanding only adult baptism is possible. The application of this ordinance to any non-responsible person destroys the New Testament meaning of the symbol. The clear New Testament evidence of this is the reason why two eminent modern theologians, the Reformed Professor Karl Barth of Basel, and the Anglican Dom Gregory Dix, have both declared in recent years, the former in 1943 and the latter in 1946, that believers' baptism is the only valid New Testament baptism. Dix says, "Christian initiation in the New Testament is described and conceived of solely in terms of a conscious adherence and response to the Gospel of God, that is, solely in terms of an *adult* initiation."[6] The believers' church requires adult baptism on the basis of a personal testimony of faith.[7]

The church therefore that is required by the New Testament understanding of faith and the way of salvation is the believers' church. This is the church that appears before our eyes in the New Testament, and which continues into the post-apostolic age. The Constantinian compromise of the fourth century put an end to this church, although it had already to some extent been compromised. The mass mixed church which followed was a lamentable descent from the high concept of the church in the New Testament. The Reformation restored the center of the Gospel but failed to restore the church to its believers' character. Neither the Catholic Church nor the main Reformation churches practiced a believers' church. On the contrary, they teamed with the governments which agreed with them in coercing the people to accept their theologies and church orders. Dissenters were imprisoned, exiled, tortured into recantations, or executed. Princes were given legal power to choose the religion they preferred for their people and to compel conformity to it. This was true in Reformation magisterial Protestantism,

Lutheran, Anglican, and Reformed, as well as in Catholicism.

The Anabaptists were the only exception to this pattern, followed later by the Church of the Polish Brethren. Though a part of the Reformation movement, they established again the believers' church, with the requirement of adult confession of faith and a commitment to follow Christ for admission to membership; and rejected all coercion by state or church in matters of faith.[8] They founded the first free church at Zurich-Zollikon in January, 1525.[9] The maintenance of the believers' church in practice is a continuing responsibility and concern for their descendants and for the free churches as a whole, which is not fulfilled merely by refusing to baptize infants. It requires a continuing living faith and responsible commitment and performance as disciples on the part of all the members all the time. Let us therefore consider the meaning of this discipleship.

Disciples

The risen Lord commanded the eleven apostles as representative of the total church to "make disciples of all nations" (Matthew 28:19). Since we accept this commission as our own we must know the meaning of discipleship in order to be able to fulfill our Lord's directive. It is the same commission as that given to the whole Pentecostal company when He said, "You shall be my witnesses." In Acts 14:21, where we are told that the apostles preached the Gospel and made many disciples in Derbe, the verb for "make disciples" is exactly the same as that in the great commission, and the passage clearly conveys the meaning that becoming a disciple is the response to the preaching of the Gospel. We of today are among those who have been made disciples by the preaching of the Gospel, and we need a guide for *our* discipleship, the church's discipleship. Let us then consider the church as a company of disciples.

For the meaning of discipleship we must turn to the Gospels, where the term "disciple" is used as the regular name for the followers of Jesus and appears some 225 times, and where Jesus states in clear terms what He expects of His disciples.

"Disciple" was a familiar term in Palestine in the time of Christ to describe those who were studying the law under the tutelage of the rabbis. The pupils of the Greek philosophers were also called disciples.[10] But Jesus' concept of discipleship was radically different from this. The rabbinical students, like the disciples of the Greek philosophers, were attached to their masters' teaching or tradition, but the disciples of Jesus were attached first of all to His person, radically and completely. Jesus did not want to be called a mere "teacher," for He was not expounding the law or explicating a code. His followers were not learners in the usual sense. They were not preparing to go on as teachers again, teaching others what they had learned. When He called upon His disciples to learn of Him, He was not speaking about ordinary learning, but about acceptance of His spirit and way of life. His disciples were to be those who believe in Him, that is, accept Him in His Messianic role as God's agent for bringing in the kingdom and submit to Him as Lord of their lives, who would adopt as their own the way of life which He exemplified and taught. The goal of Christ's disciples then and ever since has been and always will be to win other disciples to the same allegiance to their Master as Lord. This they do by making known His person and His power and by reporting the historic events linked to His life, death, and resurrection, but also by giving evidence in their own lives that He is Lord. Here Acts 1:8 and Matthew 28:19 merge. Disciples are made by witnessing, not by teaching. Preaching the Gospel is witnessing to Christ, not interpreting a law as the rabbis did, and the response is to accept Him personally as Saviour and Lord. It is a pledge to obey: to keep His commandments, to abide in His word, to do His work, and to promote His cause. All true believers are by definition disciples, for faith's commitment inevitably produces discipleship. The disciples are not a special class in the church. This title is merely another way of looking at the church. What is required of disciples is required of all.

Just as disciples attach themselves to the person of their Lord, they also attach themselves to His teachings. Therefore, the great commission includes "teaching them to observe all that I have commanded you." But the all things commanded are a way of life under the lordship of Christ, not a mere code of precepts intended to express an abstract religious philosophy, or to produce ceremonial forms or details of moral behavior. It is the way of life the Master followed—the life of compassionate love, of a serving ministry, a life deeply attached to Him and His spirit. This way of life He set forth again and again in direct teaching and in example. The promise also of the great commission, "Lo, I am with you always, to the close of the age," reflects the personal relation of disciple and Master. It is not so much a promise of assistance or comfort to working and harassed apostles or witnesses; it is a declaration that there will always be a Lord to whom the disciples can attach themselves; there will always be a Master to give them their commission and guide them; there will always be His cause to represent and His person to witness to.

Too often, in interpreting this promise, the relationship

of disciple to Lord is reversed, so that it becomes a feeling: We disciples are doing the job, but of course, we are glad to know that we can always fall back on someone to carry us through the hard spots and that there is always Someone "in the shadows keeping watch over His own." No, Christ is King Immanuel, the Captain of the hosts of the Lord, who sets the goal, who gives the marching orders, who leads the way, and with whom we are united in the power of the Holy Spirit. To stand with Him as disciples requires a complete and radical surrender to His call. Here again we see the basic relation of God to His people, both in the call and in the response. Christ comes to the world in the mighty act of the incarnation and lays claim upon us by His love through His cross and resurrection. We say "yes" to Him and are made disciples. We say, "Thou art my Lord; I will follow Thee whithersoever it take me." The life of discipleship is not narrowed down to a restrictive code; it is an abundant life of ever-widening possibilities because He whom we follow is Lord of all things, and life with Him is a boundless adventure. In this life of discipleship-adventure the disciple does not simply follow the letter of commandments but will seek creatively to apply the inner meaning of the commandments and with his fellow disciples to enter into an ever widening and intensified scope of action and experience. This becomes a sort of conversation with his Lord as to the full meaning of Christ's lordship.

The true meaning of discipleship thus is response to Christ's lordship. This response the early church made joyously and completely, whether they formally called themselves disciples or not. The earliest confession of the church was "Jesus is Lord." This was not only the ascription of divine character to Christ by the transfer to Him of the Old Testament name for God, but a declaration of Christ's royal rule over His new people of faith, and of His right to rule over all. But it was more; it was an acceptance of this rule personally by the one confessing His lordship, a pledge of allegiance and obedience. And when the whole church made the confession, it was delivering over itself body and soul to its King, to follow Him to the end, to conform to His image, to live His life after Him, to carry His rule to the ends of the earth.

Jesus' claim to lordship is indicated by His pronouncement: "All authority in heaven and on earth has been given to me" (Matthew 28:18), but also by offering His Gospel as the coming of the kingdom of God to men. This was the good news which He brought, that men could enter the kingdom by accepting Him. Kingdom, meaning reign of God, was His most all-inclusive term for the outcome of the Gospel. It meant that God will establish His rule over those who accept His gracious offer, making them disciples. The proclamation of the reign of God in the kingdom, which was the message of Christ in the Gospel, is still the message of the church of disciples. The replacement of the term "kingdom" by "church" in the epistles certainly suggests that the church is the sphere of Christ's royal reign. In other words, the church is in a real sense the kingdom which Christ announced, however much is ultimately to be included in the kingdom. Several New Testament passages actually identify the Gospel which the church preached with the kingdom. The Forty-day Gospel, as it is sometimes called, meaning the teaching of Jesus to His followers between the resurrection and ascension, was the Gospel of the kingdom, for He was "speaking of the kingdom of God" (Acts 1:3). Paul's labors in Ephesus are described as "arguing and pleading about the kingdom of God" (Acts 19:8); and his own testimony in his farewell to the Ephesian elders was that he had gone about among them "preaching the kingdom" in fulfillment of "the ministry which I received from the Lord Jesus, to testify to the gospel of the grace of God" (Acts 20:24, 25). Luke describes his two-year Roman ministry as "preaching the kingdom of God and teaching about the Lord Jesus Christ" (Acts 28:31). Paul describes redemption as being "transferred . . . to the kingdom of his beloved Son" (Colossians 1:13), and in the same epistle (4:11) refers to his colleagues as "fellow workers for the kingdom of God." To be a disciple is to be in the kingdom and to be about the King's business.

The appellation "disciple" thus fits perfectly not only with the "believers," as we have seen, but also with "people of God," and finally with "ministers of the Lord," which will be discussed in the last chapter. The unique contribution of the term "discipleship" to the understanding of the nature of the church lies precisely in the emphasis upon the lordship of Christ. The disciple follows Him in obedience, identifies himself with His cause, serves His purposes, and renounces all other loyalties. To fill in the portrait of the disciple we must take the picture which Jesus Himself gives of a disciple, as one who is "like his teacher" (Matthew 10:25), who "continues in His word" (John 8:31), who loves like his Master (John 13:34), who has the character described in the Beatitudes and the Sermon on the Mount as belonging to the "Ye" of His disciples, in fact, who fulfills all the teaching and example which He gave.

This is the vision of the church of disciples. The fulfillment of this vision will occupy the church until the end of time, as it constantly makes better disciples of its own members, as well as new disciples of all the nations.

Saints

The "saints" of the New Testament are without halos. They are not certain members who have attained a higher degree of saintliness and who are therefore on the top rung of the ladder of moral purity and piety. It was a later church, not the New Testament, that put halos on the saints. For in the New Testament all Christians are saints, once they are in the church, and they remain saints until the end unless they fall away. The Corinthian Christian community was not a paragon of perfection in any respect; in fact, Paul broadly charged them with being carnal, "men of the flesh" (I Corinthians 3:1). Yet in both his letters to Corinth he deliberately addressed them in his salutation as "saints," "called to be saints," "those sanctified in Christ Jesus." Confusion as to the meaning of "saint" in the New Testament may arise in the modern reader's mind because he is accustomed to interpret "saint" in moral terms, whereas the New Testament uses it in two senses, primarily as a status term of relation to God, and only secondarily as a description of ethical character.

The basic meaning of "saint" is "holy one," and to "sanctify" means therefore "to make holy." Exactly the same Greek root for "holy" is used in the terms Holy Spirit and holiness. Accustomed as we are to interpret "holy" in moral terms, we are inclined at once to ask: Is Paul therefore using a euphemism or deliberately flattering the Corinthians with a term not really applicable to them? Or can the Corinthians, in whatever state they were, honestly be called saints, sanctified persons? They are included in "all the saints . . . of Achaia," where apparently all Christians are meant, in the salutation of the second letter.

The problem of the meaning of "saint" goes far beyond the Corinthian letters. Paul calls the addressees in all his epistles saints. He refers to the poverty-stricken Christians in Jerusalem as "poor . . . saints" (Romans 15:26), and finally speaks of "all the churches of the saints" (I Corinthians 14:33). Twice he sends greetings from the church in which he is (Ephesus to Corinth and Rome to Philippi) in the name of "all the saints." The writer of Hebrews greets "all your leaders and all the saints" (14:24), and John the Revelator closes his book in the last verse of the Bible with the inclusive benediction, "The grace of the Lord Jesus be with all the saints" (Revelation 22:21), meaning the Christians everywhere.

The only possible conclusion from the evidence (including the fact that the word is never used in the singular) is that "saints" is simply a generic term for Christians *per se*, that is, for the members of the church.[11] But that fact does not yet explain the connotations of the word itself.

What meaning of "saint" can apply to all Christians, regardless of the degree of their ethical achievement? In what sense is the entire church a community of saints? The answer is twofold: "saint" connotes (1) a relationship of attachment to Himself which God bestows upon all His people; and (2) a binding obligation arising out of this act of God. The content of both ideas[12] is found in the meaning of the word "holy" as it is originally used in the Old Testament, referring to God and that which belongs to or is related to Him. There to be holy means to be consecrated to God and to Him alone. The holy God is the transcendent One separated from all created things, and in this sense consecrated to Himself alone. The first objective of such a God is to elect and assemble a people solely for Himself, that is, a holy people. This He accomplishes by the mighty acts by which He imparts Himself to men in judgment and mercy and operates as such a God in history. Doing this is called "sanctifying" His people. But the Old Testament emphasizes no less the sanctifying of God *by* His people. This act by the people consists of setting God apart for themselves above all other gods. In turn, the people sanctify themselves, that is, they consecrate themselves wholly to God, turning away from all other gods. This they do primarily in worship, but also by keeping God's commandments and observing His law, which is called "serving Him." Since they cannot approach God without being wholly clean, the further consequence of this sanctifying of themselves is moral purification and complete separation from all that is contrary to God's nature. Having done this they then give themselves exclusively to His service to do His will. In this concept the religious and the ethical aspects are united, although the second always is derived from the first, not vice versa. "You shall be holy, for I am holy" (I Peter 1:16; Leviticus 11:44) calls for holiness (both consecration and purification) in God's people because they are related to Him. Never were the people made God's people because they were holy. But the holy God by His very nature cannot rest until He draws men to Him to be His people, like Him in nature. "God is holy inasmuch as He imparts Himself, inasmuch as He wishes men to share in His own divine life as He brings them within the scope of His judgment and mercy. His holiness is exacting; it confronts man to pour out upon him a new life." Further: "The most intrinsic element in His being is not His wrath against sin, but His active love. The expression 'Holy' One of Israel means nothing else."[13]

We turn to the New Testament to find the very same

use of "holy." Jesus is the Holy One of God or the Holy Servant of God precisely because He is God's instrument of judgment and mercy, that is, of His love, to finally accomplish His purpose of gathering a people. He is consecrated to God for His people's sake. "For their sake I consecrate myself" (John 17:19) is His own word. The Spirit of God is likewise the Holy Spirit because He effects the regeneration and deliverance which God purposes for His people. This work of the Holy Spirit is called "sanctification" in the New Testament (II Thessalonians 2:13; I Peter 1:2), although with equal truth *God* is "he that sanctifieth" (Hebrews 2:11, KJV) and *Jesus Christ* is "our . . . sanctification" (I Corinthians 1:30). The product of God's sanctifying work is the saint, the one made "holy" by becoming a member of the people of God who are consecrated to Him alone.

The New Testament usage of "saint" or "sanctified one" carries, as "holy" does in the Old Testament, not only the idea of what God does to give His people the status of belonging to Him, but of the response of the person and people to Him. As has been stated above, God sets them apart to be His very own, but they also set themselves apart for Him. The best translation of "saints" therefore is "consecrated ones"—those set apart exclusively for God's fellowship and service.

Having now seen that the New Testament carries as the primary meaning of saint the status-relation of consecration to God, we find that the secondary meaning of purification of character is also prominent. To be set apart for God immediately implies conformity to the character of God in love and moral purity and in devotion and obedience, although the saints are not immediately by one act perfectly conformed to His character and will. This perfection they need to achieve in ever-increasing measure through growth. For this reason the appeal is made by Paul and Peter to the saints to become saintly, or by Jesus to become "perfect," to take up the yoke and learn of Him, or to take up the cross daily and follow Him. This "holy" character is the theme of urgent exhortations, in both the Gospels and the epistles, just as in the Old Testament. "If you continue in my word, you are truly my disciples" (John 8:31); "If you love me, you will keep my commandments" (John 14:15); "For just as you once yielded your members to . . . greater and greater iniquity, so now yield your members to righteousness for sanctification" (Romans 6:19); "As obedient children, do not be conformed to the passions of your former ignorance, but as he who called you is holy, be holy yourselves in all your conduct" (I Peter 1:14, 15); "But in your hearts reverence [sanctify] Christ as Lord" (I Peter 3:15); "For this is the will of God, your sanctification: that you abstain from immorality" (I Thessalonians 4:3); "For God has not called us for uncleanness, but in holiness. Therefore whoever disregards this, disregards not man but God, who gives his Holy Spirit to you" (I Thessalonians 4:7, 8); "Christ loved the church and gave himself up for her, that he might sanctify her, . . . that the church might be presented before him in splendor, without spot or wrinkle" (Ephesians 5:25-27). In these passages "sanctify" and "sanctification" have acquired the meaning of ethical perfecting: the connotation of "consecration" has almost vanished.

The meaning of the church of "saints" has now become clear. God calls and sets apart for Himself the people He loves and redeems, and His people accept this calling and consecrate themselves to Him and to His service. In their new status of consecrated men, a status made possible by grace, they strive earnestly to conform themselves to Him, to become morally clean and holy in all their conduct, to present themselves as "a living sacrifice, holy and acceptable to God," "not [to] be conformed to this world but [to] be transformed" (Romans 12:1, 2), as obedient children. Since God is always present with His people, and His people are His visible representatives among the nations, His glory must also be present in them. This glory is the glory of holiness, and the saints are in this sense also glorious. The figure of "light" also conveys the concept of holiness, and the saints must "walk in the light, as he is in the light" (I John 1:7).

In this figure of the saints again we find in essence the figure of the people of God, in which calling and response are inseparable. The added aspect now is the striving for holiness in life to match the character of Him who has called them. Thus, the saints strive to become saints. The specifications for their striving are written large on the pages of the Gospels and epistles alike. The goal is nothing less than the righteousness of God, "the upward call of God in Christ Jesus." Philippians 3:8-14.

5

THE LORD'S MINISTERS

The Mission and Ministry of the Church

It is of the very nature of the church that it has a calling and ministry in the world, and that it fulfills that calling. In this last chapter we shall consider what the calling is, and how and by what means the church shall fulfill it.

The Church's Calling to Be the Church

The first and primary calling of the church is to be the church of Christ. If it fails in this, all its ministries in the world fail. The first task of the church then is to be the new creation[1] in the midst of the old creation. It not merely proclaims the availability of redemption but demonstrates in its life what that redemption is. By its life it heralds the new reality in Christ, the new age which has broken in and which is the new hope of the world. It responds to God's great acts of reconciliation, redemption, and salvation in Christ, and becomes the sphere in which the Holy Spirit works. Thereby its life is increasingly transformed after the image of its Lord.

Paul speaks twice, with dramatic emphasis, of the new creation. In Galatians 6:15, 16 we read: "Neither circumcision counts for anything, nor uncircumcision, but a *new creation.* Peace and mercy be upon all *who walk by this rule,* upon the Israel of God [italics mine]." It is living as a new creation that makes the new Israel of God. This same conviction is expressed still more sharply in the following sentence, which I quote in Moffatt's translation: "If any one is in Christ, there is a new creation; the old has gone, the new has come" (II Corinthians 5:17). This new creation began at the resurrection but is constantly proceeding, for the church is "walking in the resurrection," to use a phrase of Menno Simons. Paul had the privilege of seeing the new creation emerging as he preached the Gospel. No wonder he could exclaim exultantly, "But thanks be to God, who in Christ always leads us in triumph. . . . For we are the aroma of Christ to God among those who are being saved" (II Corinthians 2:14, 15). The first calling of the church is to become in reality what it is by definition.

A major hindrance to the church's being the new creation is a doctrine of man which holds that original sin remains in man as such a powerful negation to the grace of God that it is really next to impossible to live the resurrection life of victory over sin; and the chief fruit of the Gospel therefore is forgiveness. On this basis there is little real expectancy of the new creation. Forgiveness then becomes the chief experience of the grace of God in the church, with a lively sense of the power of the atonement in the death of Christ. This was characteristic of much of the evangelical Reformation, particularly of Luther. As T. F. Torrance has recently put it, Luther's view really means "that the believer does not really learn to live on the resurrection side of the cross."[1a] It was the Anabaptists in particular who insisted that the grace of God does produce a new creation, that men should and can walk in newness of life on the resurrection side of the cross, and that the church is no true church of Christ if it fails at this point.[2] That there will always be a tension between what the church is and what it should be in Christ must not be forgotten, but the ideal must be maintained and striven after. No surrender to defeat is possible. The church dare not take the low road because the high road is difficult, nor may it let itself be submerged in the problematics and ambiguities of ethical decision-making.

A second hindrance to the continuing new creation by God is undue emphasis upon the church as an institution. It is all too easy to assume that maintenance of structure, offices, and forms is the most important thing in the life of the church; these then become ends in themselves instead of serving the creativity of the church. The church *is* inevitably also an institution as a necessity of her humanness, but she is first of all the reign of God's life-giving grace and Spirit.

A third hindrance to the continuance of the new creation is tradition. To be satisfied with what has been, to love the familiar, to resist change, to feel a strong bond to the past, is human. But holding too fast to tradition can thwart movement to meet the needs of today, or can so overpower the voice of the Spirit that He cannot be heard. Tradition must serve, not control. None of these hindrances are inevitable; all can be overcome.

The Calling to Witness

The second great calling of the church is to witness. "You shall be my witnesses" (Acts 1:8) were Christ's last words on earth to His disciples. Several significant meanings flow from this concept.

In the first place, the witness is to someone and something outside itself—to Christ, as indeed the quoted verse says. The church does not witness to itself; it points like John the Baptist to the Lamb of God which takes away the sin of the world.

Second, the witness is to something that has happened historically, for at the very heart of the Gospel of salvation is the series of events that constitute the total Saviorhood of Jesus Christ for us men and our salvation. Christianity is a historical religion anchored in the realities of history. This witness to history is not just for the purpose of remembrance for inspiration, precious as that is, but for making the incarnation, the atonement, and the resurrection of Christ a living present reality. Only so can their benefits be experienced in the present. The preaching of the story is for the purpose of contemporaneous, decisive confrontation of men with the living Christ, not just the memory of Him. Christ must be born unto us, as well as to them of old; and He must be born *in us.* Christ was crucified historically once for all; He does not repeat His sacrifice; He dies no more. But we die now with Him and rise with Him to newness of life. The preaching of the cross, a historic fact, is for the purpose of making Him who hung on the cross our present Saviour and Lord. The witness to Christ, therefore, is not merely a witness to the historic Christ but also, and especially, to the present living Christ. "Preaching Christ" means basically not preaching about the historic Christ, describing His character, mentioning what He did, repeating the facts of the Passion and resurrection, although all this has its place in the total round of preaching, "but speaking in such a way that the Holy Spirit can make audible and bring home the Word of God, which is Christ Himself, to the minds and consciences of contemporary men and women."[3]

In the third place, the real witness of the church to Christ lies in its living demonstration of the presence of Christ. It cannot bear witness to Christ unless it lives the life that proceeds from the source, Christ. The real presence of Christ is not in word or sacrament, which can only be symbols, or at most signs of His presence, but in His personal effect upon men. The miracle of the presence of Christ is evidenced by the miracle of the fruit of His redeeming work in the lives of people in the church. One major example is that the offer and promise of the miracle of forgiveness to broken and guilty sinners is effective and believable only if the miracle of forgiveness has been experienced in the church. "The forgiveness of God," writes H. R. Mackintosh, "is only believable" if two things are present in the church: "first, the living witness of pardoned men to the truth in which they themselves have found life and power, and secondly, the Christian habit of *practicing* forgiveness. In other words, the church is not merely a society to proclaim that loving divine pardon [is available] . . . ; it is a society in which men are accustomed to forgive each other. The second requisite is as vital as the first; without it the good news of pardon can make no impression."[4] Hendry adds: "The grace to forgive is a witness to the grace by which we are forgiven, because it is the same grace; for there is only one grace, the grace of our Lord Jesus Christ."[5]

This, then, is the witness of the church to Christ—that He is present in her midst now, that His redeeming and saving grace is working, that His love is controlling, that His lordship is operating, that His life is being reproduced. The words of the church are secondary to this. This is why the primary calling of the church is to be the church. The world must see the effect of Christ in order to believe in Christ; demonstration must accompany proclamation.

The Church's Ministry the Continuation of Christ's Ministry

The ministry and mission of the church are also presented in the New Testament, indeed by Christ Himself, as the continuation of His ministry of service. "As the Father has sent me, even so I send you" (John 20:21). Let us therefore examine Christ's ministry in order to understand the church's ministry.

Let it at once be said that the work of Christ, which has customarily been described as threefold, prophet, priest, and king, cannot be the work of the church. Historically, some churches, particularly the Roman Church, have assumed all or part of this work as their mission. But this is an impossibility, a claim without warrant in Scripture.

The church does, however, exercise a priesthood, often referred to in Protestantism as the "priesthood of all believers." The New Testament makes several explicit statements about this priesthood in I Peter 2:5, 9 and in Revelation. Christians are called "a holy priesthood," whose function is "to offer spiritual sacrifices acceptable to God through Jesus Christ," and "a royal priesthood." Praise is ascribed to Christ "who loves us and has freed us from our sins by his blood and made us a kingdom, priests to his God and Father" (Revelation 1:5, 6), and Christians are again described as "a kingdom and priests" in Revelation 5:10. Paul's appeal to the Roman Christians (Romans 12:1) to offer their bodies as a living sacrifice dedicated and fit for His acceptance implies the priesthood.

The priesthood of all believers has been variously interpreted, but unconvincingly, as the substitution of direct access to God by the individual in place of the Roman Catholic sacerdotal mediator priesthood, or again as Christians serving as priests for each other. T. W. Manson has made a strong case for understanding the priesthood of Christians to have the direct Old Testament sense of offering sacrifices to God, just as it is used in Romans 12.[6] The sacrifice of the Christian "priest" is his dedicated service to Christ and fellow men, just as Christ presented His life as a sacrifice to God for His fellow men.

The church's ministry is best understood as a direct succession to and imitation of Christ's ministry as His service of love and compassion to men, first of all on behalf of their salvation and spiritual health, but also for their other needs. For this service two Greek words are used, *douleia* and *diakonia.* A *doulos* is a "slave" and a *diakonos* is a "servant." Both words are used in the New Testament for both Christ and His disciples. Unfortunately, in the King James Version "servant" was made the translation for *doulos,* possibly because of the low status of servants in seventeenth-century England, while "minister" was used for *diakonos,* with the danger of referring this to the clergyman minister. Jesus defines His ministry in the remarkable sentence, "The Son of man . . . came not to be served but to serve" (Mark 10:45), where the verb *diakoneo* is used. Just before this He said to His disciples who were striving for the greatest posts in His kingdom: "Whoever would be great among you must be your *diakonos,* and whoever would be first among you must be *doulos* of all" (Mark 10:44).

The right translation of *doulos* is "slave," not "servant" or "minister," and it carries a very sharp meaning. A *doulos,* as the men of Christ's day in the Greco-Roman world well knew, where one third of the population were slaves, was one who was bound body and soul to his master, who served him exclusively and completely, who could never be freed from his enslavement except by the will of his master, who in fact had no will of his own and never decided what his own duties would be. To the Greeks, with their ideal of freedom, a slave was a despised person. In the Septuagint Greek translation of the O.T., therefore, *doulos* is used only for the hated slave-service of Israelites to foreign conquerors, never for service by the man of Israel to his fellow Israelite. The Israelite was called *pais* (child) if he was in servitude to his ethnic fellow. But service to God is generally represented in the Old Testament by the word *doulos*.[7] When this word then is used for Christ and Christians, its chief point is to carry the sense of complete dedication to God or to Christ in unlimited and unending service. The Greek idea of freedom from slavery, that is, not being bound to any master, is never found in the Christian usage, for the Christian knows no autonomy; he has a master. Delivery from the bondage to sin and Satan by becoming a Christian means changing masters, not becoming free from all masters. The Christian is a slave to his only Master, Christ. But in the service of Christ the Christian finds freedom precisely as a slave, because he is so identified with Christ that Christ's will becomes his own, and because he is therefore completely freed from the domination of sin. He is incidentally also free from any bondage to the ceremonial law or to fellow humans.

The counterpart to "slave" *(doulos)* is "Lord" *(kurios)*. Hence, to call Christ *kurios* was to accept the role of *doulos* to Him, even when this is not always expressly stated. But there is only one Lord; hence, Jesus' disciples are not to "lord it" over fellow disciples or fellow men, and elders are warned by Peter that they are not to be "[lording it] over God's heritage," the church. I Peter

5:3, KJV. The Christians' service to one another is therefore not called *douleia,* but *diakonia,* for Christians can be slaves only to Christ; to each other they are to be servants and brethren. The two exceptions to this are II Corinthians 4:5 and Galatians 5:13, both with special overtones. In the first reference Paul calls himself and his co-worker *douloi* of the Corinthians for Jesus' sake, thus taking on the same *doulos* spirit they (Paul) had toward Jesus. In the second reference Paul says that the brethren are not to use their freedom "as an opportunity for the flesh, but through love [to] be *douloi* of one another." The apparent reason for using *douloi* here is to contrast the improper use of freedom from the law's enslavement with real and binding commitment to service to each other; "be slaves to one another," Paul says, to avoid the dangers of freedom. When Jesus changes from calling His disciples *douloi* to "friends" (John 15:15), it is because He has introduced them to all that the "master is doing" and told them "all that I have heard from my Father." *Douloi* do not normally receive such inside information from their masters. Paul admonishes Philemon to receive his runaway slave Onesimus "no longer as a slave *(doulos)* but more than a slave, as a beloved brother" (Philemon 16).

The Christian's service is to be completely selfless service. As John Mackay has well said, the two greatest symbols of the church are the cross and the towel.[8] The one means salvation, the other service. The Christ who took the towel to wash His disciples' feet is our example in service. Paul says that Christ took the form of a *doulos* when He came to earth in the incarnation. Philippians 2:7.

Paul delighted to call himself a *doulos* of Jesus Christ. Romans 1:1; Philippians 1:1; Galatians 1:10. In the description of his ministry to the Corinthians he called himself, with his co-workers, "your *douloi* for Jesus' sake" (II Corinthians 4:5) because he wanted to emphasize their obligation to serve the believers there in complete selfless dedication. One cannot be a *doulos* of Christ if he at the same time tries to please men (Galatians 1:10), for the *doulos* is a man entirely subject to the will of his one and only *kurios*. The requirement of Jesus that those accepting His call to discipleship must first deny themselves was not a requirement for salvation but a requirement for *doulos* service.

Diakonos and its verb cognate is the word commonly used in the New Testament for servant and serving, and *diakonia* is properly translated by the Revised Standard Version as service. *Diakonos* means simply one who does work for another, who helps another, who devotes himself to another's cause, who works to meet or help meet another's physical and spiritual needs, or to accomplish what the employer or Master wants to have accomplished. So we read of *diakonoi* of God, of Christ, of the church, of the Gospel, and of righteousness. Peter admonishes the believers to serve one another (I Peter 4:10). Jesus offered Himself to His disciples as the example, for He said, "I am among you as one who serves" (Luke 22:27). The proper word for the ministry *(diakonia)* of the church would be the "service" of the church, but since "service" has been debased somewhat by its modern commercialization, "ministry" carries a better flavor. Let us now turn to the content of the church's service-ministry.

The Content of the Church's Ministry

A comprehensive survey of the total ministry and mission of the church suggests a fourfold ministry: (1) the ministry to edification of the church internally; (2) the ministry of the Gospel, that is, evangelism; (3) the ministry of good works; and (4) the ministry of the prophetic preaching of righteousness to the world. Let us now consider these four briefly.

(1) *The ministry of edification* or building up the church and its members. Paul describes this ministry in principle in Ephesians 4:11-16. "And his gifts were that some should be apostles, some prophets, some evangelists, some pastors and teachers, for the equipment of the saints, for the work of ministry, for building up the body of Christ" (Ephesians 4:11, 12). We seek in vain a more detailed description or analysis of the service which the church needs from its special servants to build itself up, beyond the brief outline given in Ephesians 4, and in I Corinthians 12 and Romans 12 in connection with the discussion of the gifts given to the church. However, something of the nature of this service can be inferred from the descriptive names given to the functions of the "some" who are special servants. There were the prophets, who made known the will of God in the new age, corresponding to the prophets of the old covenant, and who in part at least correspond to the preacher of later times and today. There were the pastors or shepherds, whose function clearly was to help individual members who needed spiritual food, counsel, comfort, reproof, and cleansing by confession and forgiveness, and who correspond to the pastor of later times and today. Then there were the teachers whom we may well suppose to have interpreted the Old Testament Scriptures in their new meaning for the new age, who pointed out application of Christian truth to the practical aspects of living, and gave ethical instruction. This function would also find its counterpart in the work of the modern pastor-preacher. In fact, some read the Ephesians phrase "pastors and

teachers" as one composite concept of pastor-teacher. The evangelist in the list of functions is the one who preached the good news of the Gospel to the unbeliever, and so had no primary ministry inside the church; he commonly served as an itinerant missionary. Noteworthy is the complete absence of the priest in the list of special servants. Noteworthy also is the lack of evidence that the church chose the special servants; they were the gift of God.

No outline is given as to precisely what the ministry of the members to each other is in the building up of each member in Christ after they have received the help of the special servants. I have described this earlier, although somewhat briefly, in the discussion of the meaning of fellowship in Chapter 3. In general, it should include all the ministries of word and life, of testimony, witness, admonition, and service, which deepen understanding and intensify experience, and enlarge the scope of action and practice in the total Christian vocation of faith, discipleship, holy living and service, so that the life of Christ is manifested in all the life of all the believers. Today this mutual ministry of the members in practice could include meetings for mutual discussion or prayer, procedures for the nurture not only of children and youth but of adults as well—the preparation of Christian literature, the training of workers for special tasks and duties, the provision of avenues of service to the material needs of the members in all forms of mutual aid, and other works. The scope of the ministry of edification in this internal ministry is large and comprehensive and in fact practically inexhaustible. It was so in apostolic times and is so today. The performance of this ministry is of course subject to the church as a body of the whole. Except for the Quakers most church groups have assigned a major role in this ministry to a special person carefully chosen and set apart (ordained), whose major function is preaching and teaching, and who is directly under the control of the church. He is in effect the successor to the apostolic prophet and teacher, and the pastor.

(2) *The ministry of the Gospel* is basically the effective presentation of the good news of God's offer in Christ to sinful men for forgiveness, reconciliation, redemption, and adoption into the family of the household of God, the church. This is the ministry of evangelism to those who have not yet come to faith in Christ. I find helpful here the insight of C. H. Dodd, who distinguishes in the apostolic preaching the *kerygma,* that is, the proclamation of the Gospel of salvation to the world outside the faith, and the *didache,* that is, the ethical teaching to those in the faith.[9] It is a distinction which we obscure all too often by our confusion of evangelism and revival. New Testament evangelism is for those outside of Christ. This is an essential ministry of the church in the world. In fact, the church exists for this purpose. It is sometimes said: The church not only has missions; she is mission. This mission is the first part of the great commission, and it is an assignment that takes the church to the ends of the world and to the end of the age.

There are reasons, however, why we may not separate too sharply the *kerygma* from the *didache.* The first reason is that the Gospel proclamation is not given in a vacuum which asks for a simple crucial momentary decision for a Yes or No. In addition to the invitation to accept the offer of God's grace it is also an invitation to discipleship. Hence this discipleship exposition is a part of the Gospel invitation. It is a faulty Gospel preaching which limits the Gospel offer to forgiveness, and does not describe the grace of God as the way to a life. Discipleship is not something which can be added afterward as a secondary but nonessential possibility, or as something for advanced Christians. When the Gospel is so understood, it is distorted. The seeking sinner is set on an erroneous course in advance, if faith in Christ is not given its full meaning as newness of life. This full Gospel can be offered without necessarily expounding at the outset all the ethical consequences of a saving faith, but it must be offered. Jesus points out the danger of not counting the cost of discipleship before answering the call. Luke 14:26-32. A faulty interpretation of the Gospel is the direct cause of the "cheap grace" concept, which Dietrich Bonhoeffer so vigorously excoriates.[10] The wrong concept of justification which is implied in "cheap grace" is often the result of faulty evangelism which finally leads to justification *in sin,* rather than justification *of the sinner,* to use Bonhoeffer's language.

The second reason why the *didache* cannot be separated too sharply from the *kerygma,* with the consequent exclusion of the *kerygma* from the internal ministry of the church, is that (1) Christians continue to live by grace through faith, the same grace which brought them salvation, and they need the continuing cleansing and forgiveness of Christ. They can profit therefore from a repeated reminder of the basis of their salvation. For renewal they do not first need moral and practical instruction; they need a renewal of their life by a fresh laying hold on their salvation. (2) The children who grow up in the nurture of the church need the knowledge of the *kerygma* as the Gospel by which they also are saved, just as do those outside the church. Our understanding of the meaning of faith and membership in the body of Christ, which we arrived at earlier in these discussions, commits us to the proposition that only responsible persons can have faith, that only those who make a deliberate commitment can be in Christ. The nurture of the church does enfold the children of the church, and parents as well as the whole church are to rear children "in the discipline and instruction of the Lord" (Ephesians 6:4). And Jesus did include children in His love. But all children, as they mature and take responsibility for their lives, need to come to conscious faith in Christ and personal commitment to discipleship to Him. In doing this the youth of Christian parents have the great advantage of the love and the nurture of the church; they need never find themselves far out in the world, but can come to faith as the call of the Gospel reaches them understandingly within the Christian community. For this reason, if for no other, the Gospel must be preached within the fellowship of the church. And, of course, unbelievers who are invited into the church meeting should hear the call of the Gospel. There is, however, a danger that must be avoided, namely, that the evangelistic call will be confused with the call to renewal, and that the needed stimulus to growth may produce a breach in Christian assurance.

Two other ministries of the church remain to be considered: *the ministry of good works,* which the love and compassion of Christ moves the members of His body to perform, and *the ministry of the prophetic word of righteousness* to the world. Jesus told His disciples, "You are the salt of the earth. . . . You are the light of the world" (Matthew 5:13-16). The light is to shine in the darkness, which in the New Testament means the world of men at enmity with God; and the salt is to be applied to the world's decaying life. The light and salt include not merely the prophetic words but also the prophetic deeds, the works which Jesus says will lead the unbelieving world as it beholds them to glorify the Father in heaven. Thus, these two ministries merge into one in their ultimate outcome: both serve the evangelistic ministry.

(3) *The ministry of good works* is an extension of Christ's ministry of good works, motivated by compassionate love for the total welfare of men whether within or without the flock of Christ. The body of Christ which represents Him in the world must represent this compassionate love also. Such love will extend the ministry of the good works of the church beyond its own borders into the total community of which it is a part locally, nationwide, and worldwide. This is not a ministry to be grudgingly tolerated and limited, but boldly and generously performed. It is not, of course, to be given to the neglect of the needs of its own members, for whom the church has a special responsibility arising out of the fellowship of faith. So Paul could rightly say, "Let us do good to all men, and especially to those who are of the household of faith" (Galatians 6:10), and emphasize "as we have opportunity." Paul also summoned the believers to "overcome evil with good," and to feed and give drink to the enemy. Romans 12:20, 21. Jesus had already given the same directives to the disciples and with even more urgency: "Love your enemies, bless them that curse you, do good to them that hate you . . . that ye may be the children of your Father which is in heaven" (Matthew 5:44, 45, KJV).[11] The second great commandment, "love your neighbor," found already in the Old Testament but interpreted before Christ to mean love for the fellow Israelite, was extended by Christ in the parable of the Good Samaritan to mean "love and serve any one in need; you are the neighbor." Christian love in this perspective of Christ means to seek the welfare of those outside the fellowship of His church, else the Chris-

tian is no better than the charitable Pharisee or the compassionate publican of Matthew 5:43-48. It was Jesus also who in almost terrifying warning words stated the possibility of final exclusion from His kingdom at the Last Judgment, declaring that failure to minister to the hungry, the thirsty, the sick, and the prisoner means failure to minister to Him. Matthew 25:41-46. His only requirement for the ministry was that it was to be in His name, that is, issuing from His love and character which dwells in His disciples. A social ministry or, as it is sometimes called, a social service, is therefore not to be rejected by the church as contrary to the Gospel, nor is it merely an option at the convenience of individuals; it is a command to the church.[12] It may in no case supplant the ministry of the Gospel in evangelism, or the ministry of edification in the church, but it is an essential ministry arising out of the very nature of the church. The church is a servant church because it has a servant Lord.

(4) *The prophetic ministry* of the proclamation of the righteousness of God to a sinful world, by word in addition to the works just mentioned, likewise has its place in the life of the church. This does not mean that the *didache* for the internal ministry of the church, which is based on acceptance of the Gospel and a living in Christ and following Him, is for an unredeemed world which does not have His indwelling Spirit. It means a proclamation of the law of righteousness which God has established and which is for the health of nations. It is not merely a proclamation of judgment to come upon ungodliness, else the church would fall under the condemnation of the unwilling prophet to Nineveh, for it is not the will of God that any should perish. There is no place in the life of the church for a punitive ministry to the world which would call

down fire from heaven upon those who will not respond, as did the sons of thunder on the way to Jericho who were rebuked by the Master. Luke 9:54, 55. But judgment will come, and is now already operative in the world of sin, and this can be pointed out. The church has the duty to put its finger on sin anywhere and everywhere, if for no other reason than as a part of its evangelism, for it is the preaching of the judgment on sin which leads to the conviction of sin and turning from it. The conscience of the sinner needs stirring to bring him to a realization of his condition. Thus in the name of God the church may be the conscience of the world, speaking to its condition from the point of view of the righteousness which is required of all men.

Who Are the Lord's Ministers?

We come now to the question of who is responsible for the ministry of the church, and how it shall be performed. Here the clarity of the Scripture has been clouded by the history of the church. The ministries of the church, both internal and external, as seen in the New Testament, are the responsibility of the whole church. All the saints are to minister according to their gifts, and all have gifts. This does not mean that every member does everything, but that each is responsible for all the ministries of the church. He shares in the support and guidance of those ministries in which he does not directly participate, and he receives the guidance and support of his co-members for his own particular part of the ministries. He does not ask, What does the church owe me? but, What do I owe my fellow members in the church, and what is my obligation, as a part of the church, to the world? It is the responsibility of the church as a whole then to see that *he* is fully ministered to according to his needs. The total church is involved in the ministry of Christ through His church.

The tragedy of the historical church is that it lost this vision. Early a differentiation arose between the ordained clergy and the rest of the membership. This was a difference not only of function but also of status, which hardened in the Roman Church into the concept that the church is the hierarchy of clergy to whom the laity is subject. In effect, the clergy then performed the ministries of the church, supported by the laity. This suppression and demotion of the laity has had tragic consequences for the life of the church, for it means the denial of the body of Christ and the fellowship of faith. It restricts the service of the members to a minimum, and it denies them any share in the guidance and control of the ministries. Hendrik Kraemer, in his excellent book, *A Theology of the Laity,*[13] has traced this historical development and shown how the demotion of the laity has led to a corruption and perversion of the concept of the nature of the church, and a corresponding corruption of the concept of the church's ministry as well as of the role of the clergy in the church. This process was paralleled by an excessive emphasis on the institutional character of the church. It has been the tragedy of state-church Protestantism and all too much of the free churches as well. A rather common attitude among Christians is to accept the church as something to attend and support, but to leave its work to be done by the clergy or by a few special persons. The clergy in turn appeal to the laity to support the church, that is, to support them and the institutionalized ministries, and end by thanking the members for attending the church and supporting it. This attitude is often strengthened, if not caused, by the non-involvement of the members in the government and guidance of the church locally and in general,[14] even when laity serve in the general councils of the church.

But it is fair to say that in the minds of many if not most members of the actual churches today this state of affairs is not only *not* reprehensible; it is an acceptable and indeed a preferable and comfortable condition. These lay-members would be embarrassed to have it changed, either because they are unwilling to pay the price of the time and energy which they much prefer to apply to their secular pursuits and to their private interests and pleasures, or because they know inwardly that they are not fit for ministering. Their spiritual emptiness and carnality would be exposed if they attempted to serve, and they fear the painful process of spiritual renewal and reorientation which would follow such exposure. They are unaware of the rewards of full discipleship and service.

The renewal of the church in order to fulfill its ministry is a matter, first of all of the effective strengthening of that union of the members with Christ which is already basically present if there is any real faith at all, but in the second place of the right understanding of the nature of the church together with a right theology of the laity. It must begin with the free and increased flow of the internal ministry of the church to its members to provide for the growth in Christ which is the goal of all the church's activity. Only in a lesser place, and not necessarily at all as the first step, is the answer a reorganization of the structure of the church or an extension of organization or an increase of activity. The main requirement is that all members see that the church must be the church and help to make it so, that they understand that the church must be in the world, that it must fulfill its Lord's commission, and that the actual life of the total membership in the real world is the major way in which the purpose of God for the world is to be accomplished.

In the endeavor of the church toward a better fulfillment of the internal ministry as well as of the external ministry, the leadership set apart by the church for special service plays a vital part. An activation of the laity with a proper understanding of the nature of the church by no means calls for the elimination of those special servants of the church whom we ordinarily call "ministers," that is, the ordained ministers. The New Testament calls for such special servants; God gives the gifts necessary for their functioning; the apostolic church had them; and the humanness of the church in its practical sociology requires them. There is no need to dispense with them or to turn to a Quaker[15] or Plymouth Brethren type of unordained ministry. Nor is there necessity for a dissolution of the general structure of the church-at-large by throwing the whole weight of its ministry on the local congregation or on cell groups within the congregation.

But it is essential that the role of the special servants conform to the nature of the church as defined above in the New Testament teaching, and that they adequately and properly fulfill their role. It is also essential that the general structure of the church as well as that of the local congregation express the true nature of the church and the right role of all its members, both clergy and laity.[16]

The right understanding of the role of the special servants of the church listed by Paul in Ephesians 4:11-13 and I Corinthians 12:27-31 includes the following points:

(1) The special servants are necessary.

(2) They have functions, rather than offices, and several functions may be combined in one person.

(3) Not all members are qualified for these functions, for they require gifts which the Spirit bestows and which are then manifested in the life of the church, to be discovered by the body as a whole.

(4) A major function of certain special servants is to equip the members to perform their part in the total ministry of the church. These are the apostles, prophets, teachers, and pastors. Acts 13:1; Romans 12:6, 7; I Corinthians 12:28; Ephesians 4:11.

(5) The special servants are *servants* and not *lords* of the church, that is, they minister rather than exercise authority.

(6) There are special servants for evangelism, who are the itinerant preachers of the Gospel, working primarily out in the world, that is, missionaries, called in the New Testament "evangelists": Stephen, Philip, Timothy. Acts 7; 21:8; II Timothy 4:5.

Those leaders of the church who are called elders and bishops appear as a type of special servants who are really officeholders. They were chosen or appointed for supervision locally or generally. Their offices are not included in the lists of gifts and functions given in Ephesians and I Corinthians, but they are reported in the Book of Acts and elsewhere as present in the New Testament churches.[17] Here we must speak of offices and not just functions.

Jesus did not appoint any special servants, not even elders. He did appoint apostles to be the general leaders of the church, but He did not order any particular structure of church organization or offices. Nor is there any indication that the organizational pattern of the earliest churches must be the pattern through all ages. If it were so, we should be able to find the appropriate commands or at least a clear and complete pattern. However, any structure of organization of offices adopted later dare not violate or harm the essential nature of the church as we have found it in the direct teachings of Jesus and in the inspired writings of the apostles. He gave the Spirit to guide the church in this matter as in others, for the Spirit was to guide His people "into all truth," and such guidance did not cease with the apostolic church, but continues.

The ministry of the special servants of the church should be understood as in reality a representational ministry. It is performed not only on behalf of the church, but also in the name of the church. The Gospel which is preached is the Gospel entrusted to the church as a whole and in turn entrusted by it to the evangelist. The sermons of the preacher shall speak the mind of the church about the content of the Scriptural exposition, the imperatives of the Christian ethic, the counsels of comfort and consolation, the challenge to service. When the minister speaks and serves, he is not only the agent but also the representative of the church. The church, on this ground, has the right and duty to define the content of its faith and response, which the minister in turn expounds, elaborates, and applies. The man in the pew should be able to say, in effect, to his representatives in the pulpit: You are speakers for me; what you say is my faith. This in no way diminishes the need for the special servants to exercise their special gifts, to lead the church in its faith and service, and to speak prophetically for God and His Word. Nor does it deny the need for creativity on their part, or restrict their freedom to "reprove, rebuke, and correct." And it does not need to make the preacher the "hireling" of the laity.

Indeed, the special servant has two sources for his call, commission, and authority; one is God direct and one is the church. Paul's declarations on the first source are emphatic. God acts to appoint some as apostles, prophets, teachers, pastors, and evangelists. I Corinthians 12:28; Ephesians 4:11. The gifts which enable one to prophesy, another to teach, and a third to exhort come from God, not from the church. Romans 12:6-8.

For its effective functioning the church, local and general, needs leaders. Such leadership is clearly indicated in the Acts and in the Epistles. It is also necessary from the human and sociological point of view. In the long run the quality of the church's life and service is directly dependent upon the quality of its leadership. The effectiveness of this leadership depends in turn not only upon its spiritual and personal competence but also upon the authority which the church gives to it. Ordination is a symbol of the grant of leadership and authority by the church.

The mission and ministry of the church in the world is a great task which requires the participation of the total membership until the end of the age. It is the business of the leadership of the church to enlist all in the ministry of the church that its mission may be accomplished. It is the obligation and privilege of all the members to share fully in this ministry according to the Spirit's gifts to them, for such a sharing is of the very essence of the church, and only thus can God's purpose in the world be accomplished.

It is God's purpose that His love and power in grace and redemption be made known by the church until the end of history, that the church stand as a witness to Christ as Saviour and Lord, that it be His agent in bringing men to Christ and in fighting the battle against the powers of the enemy. This church will not be overthrown, for it is the church of God in Christ. Matthew 16:18. One day Christ will present this His church faultless before the presence of God's glory with exceeding joy. Jude 24.

9

POSTSCRIPT ON THE CHURCH AND THE WORLD

The New Testament vision of the church in the world is characterized by a singular duality. Jesus describes His disciples as those "whom thou gavest me out of the world" (John 17:6), but declares He does "not pray that thou shouldst take them out of the world" (John 17:15). "They are not of the world, even as I am not of the world," He says, yet He continues, "As thou didst send me into the world, so I have sent them into the world" (John 17:16, 18). The world from which Christ redeems us is "the present evil age" according to Paul (Galatians 1:4), and those who are redeemed are not to be conformed to it. Romans 12:2. The world hates His disciples, says Jesus, and they will have tribulation in it. John 17:14 and 16:33. They dare not love it. I John 2:15. But they are commissioned to go everywhere into it and make disciples. Matthew 28:19.

Behind this duality lies the concept of the two kingdoms. The one is "the dominion of darkness," the kingdom of this world; the other is "the kingdom of his beloved Son." To enter the church is to be delivered from the one and transferred into the other. Colossians 1:13. Thus the church is distinct from the world, not of it. It is the realm of redemption, the realm in which the Holy Spirit operates and Christ is Lord. In the New Testament the line of distinction between the two kingdoms is sharply drawn, the church and its members are separate from the world, yet operating redemptively in it to bring men to faith in Christ that they may be redeemed and incorporated into the fellowship of the body of Christ.

The two-kingdom relationship as outlined above has been broken in two opposite directions in the history of the church. On the one hand, as a result of the Constantinian compromise in the fourth century the line between church and world disappeared, and the concept of Christendom as the *Corpus Christianum* replaced it. In effect the world as such disappeared, and the patterns of culture became the patterns of Christian living. This concept continued to dominate not only medieval Catholicism both East and West, but also the state churches which emerged from the Reformation. These latter carried no mission into the world to make disciples, bound as they were by the territorial concepts of magisterial Protestantism. In the opposite direction various groups of earnest Christians down through the ages, including the free churches emerging in the Reformation and in the century following it, as well as certain modern groups, have been inclined to draw the line of separation between church and world so sharply as to retreat from the world into a sectarian isolation. These groups have been "not of the world" indeed, but also, alas, often not "in the world." Their temptation has been to "pass by on the other side" like the priest and Levite in the story of the Good Samaritan, leaving the world to perish in its misery while drawing the cloaks of their righteousness about them. The Anabaptists of the Reformation time were an exception, with their strong urge to fulfill the Great Commission. And in modern times it is these free churches which have been the pioneers in missionary outreach. Isolationism developed in the intervening centuries.

The mission of the church as presented in the fifth chapter of my book requires that it be in the world, identifying itself in a compassionate ministry with the world's needs, bearing its burdens, suffering with it. Spiritual isolationism is intolerable in the church of Christ. Whatever measures it may need to take to maintain its consecration to God and its obedience to Christ, and to keep itself unspotted from the sin of the world, these dare not constitute a wall between it and the world. The church saves its life by losing it. Its true calling lies in maintaining the duality of its relationship to the world which the New Testament teaches so clearly and powerfully, in the world but not of it.

FOOTNOTES

CHAPTER 1—*The People of God*

1 The "last days" is an eschatological concept, meaning primarily the last stages of God's redemptive work, and only in a minor sense the chronologically last days of time.

2 The crucifixion is viewed in the Pentecostal sermon and throughout Acts as the decisive act of rejection of the Messiah by the Jewish nation through the official action of the Sanhedrin. In John 1:11 the rejection is generalized, while in Jesus' words in Matt. 21:43 it is represented as the rejection of the Messianic message and program. In any case the clear position of the early church that the Jewish nation had been displaced by the church as the people of God is sharply given. There is no hint of any kind that this displacement is only temporary, and that the church is an afterthought as a provisional act of God.

3 The term is used 29 times in Acts as the name for Christians. Acts 6:1, 2, 7; 9:1, 19, 25, 26, 26, 38; 11:26, 29; 13:52; 14:20, 22, 28; 15:10; 16:1; 18:23, 27; 19:1, 9, 30; 20:1, 7, 30; 21:4, 16, 16. It is never used in the epistles and following books.

4 See Karl Ludwig Schmidt, *The Church* (London, 1950), translated from Kittel's *Theologisches Wörterbuch*. See also R. W. Kicklighter, "The Origin of the Church," in *What Is the Church*, ed. by Duke K. McCall (Nashville, 1958), pp. 28-45. The English word "church," and its parallels in other languages, comes from the Greek work *kyriakon,* meaning "belonging to the Lord," which appears twice in the New Testament.

5 Since for Israel religious, ethnic, and political aspects of the people of God were merged into one, *ecclesia* did carry more than a religious import. It could refer to any part of the people assembled for any purpose, in peace or war, worship or civil assembly.

6 Paul S. Minear, *Images of the Church in the New Testament* (Phila., 1960), pp. 82, 90.

7 It should be emphasized that the *ecclesia* of the New Testament cannot be understood solely in terms of the Old Testament. The aspect of continuity between the two testaments cannot override the decisive newness of the church. The decisive and determining factor in the New Testament is Christ Jesus. Apart from Him there can be no Christian Church. The *ecclesia* is not simply another Jewish sect. There is both continuity and discontinuity between the old Israel and the New Israel or Church.

8 For the idea of the Old Testament remnant and its application to the church, see John Bright, *The Kingdom of God* (New York, 1953), pp. 86-92, 123-26, 225-30, *et passim;* T. W. Manson, *The Teaching of Jesus* (Cambridge, 1931), pp. 175-96; the article "Remnant" in *Theological Wordbook of the Bible,* Alan Richardson, ed. (New York, 1950) and in *A Companion to the Bible,* J. J. von Allmen, ed. (New York, 1958).

9 Minear, *op. cit.,* p. 78, citing in footnote 10, Harold Sahlin, "The New Exodus of Salvation," in *The Root of the Vine,* Anton Fridericksen, ed. (London, 1953), pp. 81-95.

10 Minear, *op. cit.*, p. 69. Minear claims that the correlative idea of God's election is more important in the N.T. than the idea of the remnant (p. 81 f.).

11 Krister Stendahl, "The Called and the Chosen: An Essay on Election," in *The Root of the Vine*, pp. 63-80. "Election in Christ not only constitutes a new society; its meaning is to be found in a new society and not in the status of individuals" (p. 69), cited by Minear, *op. cit.*, p. 274. For the idea of election see von Allmen, *op. cit.*, article "Elect." This is not to deny the election of individuals conditioned upon their response and God's foreknowledge.

12 Claude Welch, *The Reality of the Church* (New York, 1958), emphasizes the character of the church as a responding people. The first section of his chapter on the people of God is entitled "A Responding People" (pp. 42-48). Note his statement, "On the contrary, however, these passages are important precisely because they express what is taken for granted throughout the New Testament, that the church is patently and indisputably (we might even say, first of all) a human community responding" (p. 46). My own discussion owes much to Welch at this point, and echoes of his thought will be noted in my phraseology.

13 See the articles "Covenant" and "Elect" in von Allmen, *A Companion to the Bible*. The idea that God is faithful to His covenant is sometimes used to support the idea of the irrevocability of His commitment to the historical ethnic people of Israel. When the facts of the history of Israel are held up to correct this interpretation, refuge is taken in the concept of an interruption of the covenant relationship of Israel by the interim insertion of the church, with the expectation of a future restoration of the covenant privileges to ethnic Israel. Apart from the fact that the New Testament knows of no such interpretation of history, this point of view ignores the doctrine of the remnant being fulfilled in the church, as well as the fulfillment of the covenant in the spiritual experience of the remission of sins. This is Peter's interpretation of the covenanted promise. Acts 2:38, 49. It is worthy of note that the modern leader of the dispensationalist school of thought, L. S. Chafer, finally is forced to profess that God has two ways of salvation, one for the Jew and one for the church, and that the church and Israel shall continue as two separate entities throughout all eternity, the former in heaven and the latter on earth. See L. S. Chafer, *Dispensationalism*, revised ed., (Dallas Seminary Press, Dallas, Texas, 1951).

14 Kurt Aland, *Die Säuglingstaufe im Neuen Testament und in der alten Kirche. Eine Antwort an Joachim Jeremias* (Munich, 1961). This notable and convincing study is a direct refutation of the position taken by Joachim Jeremias in his book, *Die Kindertaufe in den ersten vier Jahrhunderten* (1958) and published in the United States under the title *Infant Baptism in the First Four Centuries* (Phila., Westminster, 1961). Aland believes "that on the basis of the sources his total result, that infant baptism . . . was certainly demonstrable only from the third century forward, cannot be refuted."

15 Welch, *op. cit.*, p. 48.

16 K. L. Schmidt, *The Church*, p. 67.

17 See R. J. Smithson, *The Anabaptists, Their Contribution to Our Protestant Heritage* (London, 1935); F. H. Littell, *The Anabaptist View of the Church* (2nd ed., Boston, 1958); H. S. Bender, "The Anabaptist Vision," in *The Recovery of the Anabaptist Vision*, G. F. Hershberger, ed. (Scottdale, 1957), particularly pp. 37-43.

CHAPTER II—*The Body of Christ*

1 The best exegetical study of the body-concept is Ernest Best, *One Body in Christ. A study in the Relationship of the Church to Christ in the Epistles of*

the Apostle Paul (London, 1955). See also Chapter VI, "The Body of Christ," in Paul Minear's *Images of the Church in the New Testament* (Phila., 1960), pp. 174-220; also Chapter V, "The Body of Christ," in Claude Welch's *The Reality of the Church* (New York, 1958), pp. 147-88. I follow these writers in understanding the term as a symbolical figure, and not to be taken literally, realistically, or ontologically (Best, p. 112, "The phrase is not used realistically and ontologically but metaphorically") as does J. A. T. Robinson in his *The Body, A Study in Pauline Theology* (London, 1952) and as does E. L. Mascall in his *Christ, the Christian and the Church. A study of the Incarnation and Its Consequences* (New York, 1946). Accordingly, the idea of the church as an extension of the incarnation, which is held particularly in Anglican high-church theology, finds no echo in my interpretation. See Welch's argument against the realistic and incarnational view, *op. cit.*, pp. 180-88. See also Lesslie Newbigin, *The Household of God* (New York, 1954), Chapter 3, "The Body of Christ," pp. 61-93, and the article "Body" in *A Theological Wordbook of the Bible*, Alan Richardson, ed. (New York, 1951).

2 The major passages in order of importance are: I Cor. 12:12-27; Rom. 12:4, 5; I Cor. 10:16, 17; 11:29; 5:29, 30; Col. 1:17-20, 24; 2:18, 19; Eph. 1:22, 23; 4:11-16.

3 J. A. T. Robinson, *op. cit.*, p. 11 ff.; Ernest Best, *op. cit.*, "Corporate Personality and Racial Solidarity," pp. 203-7.

4 See Karl Barth, *Christ and Adam. Man and Humanity in Romans 5* (New York, 1957); Ernest Best, *op. cit.*, Chapter II, "Adam and Christ," pp. 34-43.

5 Note Welch's discussion on "Incorporation-Participation in Christ," pp. 151-64, to which I owe much.

6 Welch, *op. cit.*, p. 154.

7 Welch, *op. cit.*, p. 157.

8 Welch, *op. cit.*, p. 158.

9 The ideas in this section are drawn from Welch even though not directly quoted.

10 The "body" image is connected with the unity of the church either directly or in the following passages: I Cor. 6:15; 10:16 f.; 11:29; 12:12-27; Eph. 2:13-22; 3:6; 4:4; 4:11-16; Col. 2:9-19; 3:5. (See Welch, p. 149.)

11 By this phrase is meant that the grace of God works in and through the church to bring men to faith in Christ, the basis upon which God then works out redemption.

12 The original Latin phrase, *extra ecclesiam nulla salus,* which is attributed to Cyprian, bishop of Carthage in North Africa (d. 258), carried the meaning that no eternal salvation can be secured except through the channel of the sacramental grace conferred through the priesthood and hierarchy. I use it here to mean that God's redemptive work for men is carried on through the channel of the church by its proclamation of the Gospel and all its ministry to those who come to faith in Christ.

13 Many of the current Christian denominations are not in the true sense schisms, but have their roots in differing ethnic, geographical, or political backgrounds. The term "division" is here used only to indicate that they are now separated from one another as parts of the one body of Christ.

14 L. S. Thornton's outstanding work, *The Common Life in the Body of Christ* (London, 1942), is an extraordinarily competent and rich exposition of the concept of *koinonia.*

CHAPTER III—*The Holy Community*

1 The implications of the image of the body of Christ have already been drawn in the previous chapter, hence there will be some unavoidable overlapping with the present chapter. James Gustafson's recent book, *Treasure in Earthen Vessels. The Church as a Human Community* (New York, 1961), came to my attention only after the manuscript for my book was completed. Claude Welch calls it "A superb statement of a theme indispensable to any adequate understanding of the Christian community—the humanness of the church." I have profited much at this point from Welch's own book, *The Reality of the Church* (New York, 1950), as the careful reader of my book will observe. Welch also emphasizes strongly the humanness of the church. I do not use the term community in its precise modern sociological usage, which limits it to a geographical area.

2 See the article "Koinonia" in Kittel's *Theologisches Wörterbuch,* Vol. III (Stuttgart, 1938). L. S. Thornton, *The Common Life in the Body of Christ* (Westminster, England, 1942), is a profound and at times deeply moving discussion of the meaning of N.T. *Koinonia.* See also Roy D. Roth's Master's paper at Princeton Theological Seminary ca. 1943, "Koinonia in the New Testament."

3 Luther's translation of the New Testament into German uses *Gemeinde* for *ecclesia* in every case but one.

4 The original Greek uses the definite article with *ecclesia.* The absence of the definite article in the English translation, and the editorial insertion of an unwarranted comma, gives the impression that the *apostles'* fellowship is the meaning of the original, but the Greek does not give this impression.

5 Many have too quickly assumed that the accounts in Acts 2:44 and 4:32-35, which use the expression "had all things in common," report a case of Christian communism. A careful examination of the full accounts, however, makes it clear that no communism of production or consumption was ever established in Jerusalem. A common eating arrangement for certain persons was established, and the needy had their needs met out of an apostolic treasury into which members of the church made contributions as they were moved. The epistles likewise report no common ownership of property but imply private ownership, with individual members contributing to the needs of the poor, as well as to the general support of the church, out of their private resources.

6 As a passing historical footnote it should be remarked that a similar intensity of spiritual oneness in the Anabaptist movement of the Reformation period resulted in a similar sense of common responsibility for the material needs of all in the brotherhood. The Anabaptist mutual economic sharing was not dictated by a mere literalism in following the example of the Jerusalem church in Acts, but by an overwhelming sense of brotherhood and mutual love in the midst of the urgent needs resulting from the severe persecution by the state churches. The Hutterian Anabaptists brought this to radical expression in the Christian communism of their *Bruderhof* society, which went far beyond the practice of the Jerusalem church, which, after all, had only a relief program supported by cash contributions motivated by love, not a communistic structure. (See Robert Friedmann, *Hutterite Studies,* Goshen, Ind., 1961.) For a general treatment see R. J. Smithson, *The Anabaptists* (London, 1935). F. H. Littell, *The Anabaptist View of the Church,* 2nd ed., (Boston, 1958), and pertinent articles in the *Mennonite Encyclopedia* (Scottdale, 1955-59). George H. Williams, *The Radical Continental Reformation* (Phila., 1962), appeared after this volume was in press.

7 In recent years eagerness for renewal has led to the formation of small *koinonia* groups in various communities, called by various names such as "cell groups," "house churches," etc. The older "prayer meeting" was actually such a fellowship group. See J. L. Casteel, *Spiritual Renewal Through Personal Groups* (New York, 1957). It should be noted that well-functioning smaller fellowship groups can produce a more vital fellowship in an entire larger group than a poorly functioning small congregation. Size is not the final determining factor. In fact the experience of a larger local over-arching fellowship transcending all smaller groups can be a distinct advantage. All small "cell-groups" or other forms of grouping carry in them the seeds of individualism, exclusiveness, narrowness, and group pride; Christian love can be transformed by them into simple human possessiveness or warm friendship, although this need not be the case.

8 Lesslie Newbigin, *The Household of God* (New York, 1954), p. 55.

9 See Floyd V. Filson, *Jesus Christ, the Lord* (Phila., Westminster, 1956), p. 209 f.

10 Robert T. Handy, *Members One of Another* (Phila., 1959), p. 32. Various echoes from Handy will be found in the following section.

11 Handy, *op. cit.,* p. 33.

12 Donald G. Miller, *The Nature and Mission of the Church* (Richmond, 1957), p. 82. Cited by Handy, *op. cit.,* p. 34.

13 Newbigin, *op. cit.,* p. 97. Cited by Handy, *op. cit.,* p. 34.

14 H. Wheeler Robinson, *The Christian Experience of the Holy Spirit* (New York, 1928), p. 16. Cited by Handy, *op. cit.,* p. 37.

CHAPTER IV—*Believers, Disciples, and Saints*

1 The absence in the first cited passage of a direct reference to faith or believing is made good by Peter's statement in the second cited passage. The other references in Acts to cases of baptism all make clear that believing preceded baptism.

2 The interpretation of baptism as an act on God's part might conceivably apply in a case of adult baptism, where a responding faith with commitment can be present. In the case of nonresponsible persons such as infants, it is difficult to conceive of how God's grace can act in baptism except in a magical way. The infant is incapable of any response; but religion is a two-way communication between man and God. To substitute infant consecration or dedication for baptism is no improvement. In the strict sense, no one human being can consecrate another to God. Self-consecration is the only possible real consecration at any age, and this is possible only for responsible persons. Parents may dedicate themselves to the Christian nurture of their children; they cannot determine in advance the faith or vocation of a child without violating freedom and responsibility.

3 For a careful discussion of the meaning of *sumphutoi,* see Ernest Best, *One Body in Christ* (London, 1955), p. 51 f.

4 T. C. Smith, "The Doctrine of Baptism in the New Testament," in *What Is the Church,* Duke McCall, ed. (Nashville, 1958), p. 71. Observe the word "merely" in the first sentence of the quotation. Smith is obviously using "participation" here in the sense of status justification. The pattern of thought in my own discussion uses participation or solidarity in a dynamic sense which goes beyond "mere" justification, and *requires* participation in Christ's triumph

as a cause of the believer's triumph. Welch's interpretation of "in Christ" (*op. cit.*, p. 152) is helpful here. "It is not just a dying and rising like Christ but a sharing in His own death and resurrection." The question is not whether the Christian experience is one of status or power, but whether in addition to status it is also one of power.

5 Dietrich Bonhoeffer, *The Cost of Discipleship* (rev. ed., New York, 1959).

6 Dom Gregory Dix, *The Theology of Confirmation in Relation to Baptism* (New York, 1946), p. 31; quoted by T. C. Smith, *op. cit.*, p. 63. Karl Barth's epochal repudiation of infant baptism as contrary to the essential nature of New Testament faith is found in *The Teaching of the Church Regarding Baptism* (London, 1959). Barth says here (p. 42), for instance: "Baptism is in the New Testament in every case the indispensable answer to an unavoidable question by a man who has come to faith."

7 The testimony of faith is more than a confession of belief, being the report of experience backed by life. The substitution of the godparents' answers to the baptismal questions in the ritual of infant baptism can have no validity in this respect. The use of such a formula, in fact, indicates that basically, after all, valid answers ought to be required.

8 See Franklin H. Littell, *The Anabaptist View of the Church* (2nd ed., Boston, 1958). T. D. Price's chapter on *What Is the Church,* "The Anabaptist View of the Church," epitomizes Littell. See footnote 6 of Chapter III.

9 Fritz Blanke, *Brothers in Christ: The History of the Oldest Anabaptist Congregation, Zollikon, near Zürich, Switzerland* (Scottdale, 1961).

10 See article "Mathetes" in Gerhard Kittel, *Theologisches Wörterbuch zum Neuen Testament,* IV (Stuttgart, 1942).

11 In Phil. 4:21, the singular phrase "every saint in Christ Jesus" is equivalent to the plural. "Saints" occurs sixty-one times in the New Testament, exclusive of Matt. 27:52, where the reference is to persons coming out of their graves at the time of the crucifixion.

12 See the discussion of the idea of holiness by P. Bonnard in his article "Holy" in *A Companion to the Bible,* J. J. von Allmen, ed. (New York, 1958).

13 The two quotations are from P. Bonnard, *op. cit.*

CHAPTER V—*The Lord's Ministers*

1 The "new creation" is of course the work of God the creator through Christ, and is tied to the resurrection. But it also reaches back to the very beginning of time and of the history of Israel, with cosmic reference. Minear (*op. cit.*, pp. 105-35) has pointed out the many images related to this basic cosmic concept.

1a T. F. Torrance, *Kingdom and Church: A Study in the Theology of the Reformers* (London, 1956), p. 72.

2 Menno Simons' first book, *The Spiritual Resurrection* (1536), defines this resurrection in the opening sentence as "resurrection from sin and death to a new life." Conrad Grebel, the founder of Swiss Anabaptism, in his letter to Müntzer of September, 1524, defines the meaning of baptism thus: "It means that one had died, and should die, to sin, and walk in newness of life." The Grüningen (Switzerland) Anabaptists, in their declaration to the Zürich Council in 1527, characterized the believers as those "who have died to the will of the flesh and are now walking in the will of the spirit. . . . Those who walk therein, they are the church of Christ and the body of Christ and the Christian Church." These and numerous other supporting quotations from Anabaptist sources are found in Harold S. Bender, "Walking in the Resurrection: The Anabaptist Doctrine of Regeneration and Discipline," *Mennonite Quarterly Review,* XXXV (1961), pp. 96-110.

3 A. R. Vidler, *Christian Belief* (New York, 1950), p. 79; quoted in George S. Hendry, *The Gospel of the Incarnation* (Phila., 1958), p. 164.

4 H. R. Mackintosh, *The Christian Experience of Forgiveness* (London, 1927), p. 276 f. Quoted by Hendry, *op. cit.*, p. 170.

5 Hendry, *op. cit.*, p. 170.

6 T. W. Manson, *Ministry and Priesthood: Christ's and Ours* (Richmond, 1958), particularly pp. 70-72.

7 See the treatment of both *doulos* and *diakonos* in Kittel's *Theologisches Wörterbuch,* Vol. II (Stuttgart, 1935).

8 John A. MacKay.

9 C. H. Dodd, *The Apostolic Preaching and Its Development* (New York, 1944). "Kerygma" is the content of the message which the Lord entrusts to His herald (Kerux) to deliver. It is only from the context that the actual content of the message is known.

10 Dietrich Bonhoeffer, *op. cit.*, p. 35 ff.

11 The RSV translation at this point omits the second and third injunctions contained in the KJV, based upon the best manuscript evidence. But the parallel passage in Luke 6:27, 28 contains them.

12 The term "Social Gospel" is historically used to refer to a type of thought which in essence substituted social reform for the Gospel message of forgiveness and reconciliation by faith in Christ. That social service can be performed in a purely secular spirit ought not prevent Christians from a social service ministry which flows from Christian compassion after the example of Christ as one of the fruits of faith and the Gospel.

13 Hendrik Kraemer, *A Theology of the Laity* (Phila., 1958). It is strange that in his review of the lay movements in church history Kraemer overlooked the Anabaptist movement of the Reformation period, one of the most significant of all.

14 A number of recent writers, in addition to Kraemer, have emphasized the need for a restoration of the ministry of the laity, if the church is to be renewed. Among them is Robert A. Raines, *New Life in the Church* (Harper, 1961), particularly Chapter XI, "The Lay Ministry Emerges." See also the writings of Elton Trueblood, particularly his latest, *The Company of the Committed* (Harper, 1961).

15 See D. Elton Trueblood, *The Paradox of the Quaker Ministry* (The 1960 Quaker Lecture of the Indiana Yearly Meeting). Trueblood proposes a variation from the old type of Quaker Ministry which he considers inadequate.

16 The view that the only meaning of the church in the New Testament is the local congregation is not defensible from the New Testament text. Theologically it is also indefensible on the basis of a true understanding of the church as the people of God or the body of Christ. The congregationalistic theory, while containing an essential truth, can in its extreme form deny the very nature of the church by cutting off a geographically organized unit from full interaction with the life of the total body of the church. It can also be in reality a species of group individualism which refuses to submit itself to the counsel and authority of the general church. Certainly to use the phrase about the "two or three . . . gathered together" (Matt. 18:20) as a support for congregationalistic individualism is an exaggeration of the import of the passage.

17 Deacons appear in the Pastoral Epistles as another permanent office. Although their specific function is nowhere stated, the inference has been drawn from the appointment of the seven in Acts 6, whose successors they are presumed to be, that they ministered in the area of material needs to the poor in the church.

A LIST OF RECENT WRITINGS ON THE NATURE OF THE CHURCH

Oswald T. Allis: *Prophecy and the Church. An Examination of the Claim of Dispensationalists That the Christian Church Is a Mystery Parenthesis Which Interrupts the Fulfillment to Israel of the Kingdom Prophecies of the Old Testament* (Phila.: Presbyterian and Reformed Publishing Company, 1945), 339 p.

Believers Church, Proceedings of the Study Conference on August 23-25, 1955. (General Conference Mennonite Church, Newton, Kans., 1955), 246 p.

Harold S. Bender: "Church," in *Mennonite Encyclopedia,* I (Scottdale: Herald Press, 1955).

——: *The Anabaptist Vision* (Scottdale: Herald Press, 1961), *Mennonite Quarterly Review,* XVIII (1944), pp. 3-24, which was in turn a slightly revised version of the original publication in *Church History,* XIII (1944), pp. 3-24. Also published in *Recovery of the Anabaptist Vision* (see below in this list, Guy F. Hershberger, ed.).

——: "The Mennonite Conception of the Church and Its Relation to Community Building," *Mennonite Quarterly Review,* XIX (1945), pp. 90-100.

——: "The Usage of the term 'Church' in the New Testament," *Gospel Herald* LI (Jan. 7, 1958), pp. 1, 2, 21.

Ernest Best: *One Body in Christ. A Study in the Relationship of the Church to Christ in the Epistles of the Apostle Paul* (London: S.P. C. K., 1955), 250 p.

Dietrich Bonhoeffer: *Life Together* (New York: Harper, 1954), 122 p. A translation of *Sanctorum Communio, Eine Dogmatische Untersuchung zur Soziologie der Kirche* (Munich: Christian Kaiser, 1954).

John Bright: *The Kingdom of God. The Biblical Concept and Its Meaning for the Church* (Nashville: Abingdon-Cokesbury, 1953), 288 p.

Robert McAfee Brown: *The Significance of the Church* (Phila.: Westminster, 1957), 196 p.

Emil Brunner: *The Misunderstanding of the Church* (Phila.: Westminster, 1953), 132 p.

L. A. Champion: *The Church of the New Testament* (London: Carey-Kingsgate, 1951), 135 p.

The Church. A Symposium. J. B. Watson, ed. (London: Pickering & Inglis, 1949), 230 p.

Joseph B. Clower, Jr.: *The Church in the Thought of Jesus* (Richmond: John Knox, 1959), 160 p.

G. A. Danell: "The Idea of God's People in the Bible," *Root of the Vine, Essays in Biblical Theology,* Anton Fridrichsen, ed. (New York: Philosophical Library, 1953), pp. 23-36.

Suzanne de Dietrich: *The Witnessing Community. The Biblical Record of God's Purpose* (Phila.: Westminster, 1958), 180 p.

R. N. Flew: *Jesus and His Church. A Study of the Idea of the Ecclesia in the New Testament* (New York: Abingdon, 1938), 275 p.

———, ed.: *The Nature of the Church.* Papers Presented to the Theological Commission Appointed by the Continuation Committee of the World Conference on Faith and Order (New York: Harper, *ca.* 1952), 347 p.

P. T. Forsyth: *The Church and the Sacraments* (London: Independent Press, 1955; 1st ed., 1917), 308 p.

Reginald H. Fuller: "Church," *A Theological Wordbook of the Bible,* Alan Richardson, ed. (New York: Macmillan, 1951).

James Leo Garrett: "The Nature of the Church According to the Radical Continental Reformation," *Mennonite Quarterly Review,* XXXII (1958), pp. 111-27.

James M. Gustafson: *Treasure in Earthen Vessels. The Church as a Human Community* (New York: Harper, 1961), 141 p.

Robert T. Handy: *Members One of Another. Studies in the Nature of the Church as It Relates to Evangelism* (Phila.: Judson Press, 1959), 114 p.

A. G. Hebert: *The Throne of David, a Study of the Fulfillment of the Old Testament in Jesus Christ and His Church* (London: Faber and Faber; New York: Morehouse-Gorham Co., 1941), p. 277.

Guy F. Hershberger, ed.: *The Recovery of the Anabaptist Vision* (Scottdale: Herald Press, 1957), 360 p. This volume contains among others the following pertinent essays:

H. S. Bender, "Anabaptist Vision"; F. H. Littell, "The Anabaptist Concept of the Church"; J. L. Burkholder, "The Anabaptist Vision of Discipleship"; J. W. Fretz, "Brotherhood and the Economic Ethic of the Anabaptists"; Robert Friedmann, "The Doctrine of the Two Worlds"; Paul Peachey, "The Modern Recovery of the Anabaptist Vision."

George Laird Hunt: *Rediscovering the Church* (New York: Association Press, 1956), 178 p.

Daniel Jenkins: *The Strangeness of the Church* (Garden City: Doubleday, 1955), 188 p.

George Johnston: *The Doctrine of the Church in the New Testament* (New York: Macmillan, 1943), 156 p.

Hendrik Kraemer: *A Theology of the Laity* (Phila.: Westminster, 1958), 191 p.

R. B. Kuiper: *The Glorious Body of Christ* (Grand Rapids, 1958?), 383 p.

Franklin H. Littell: *The Anabaptist View of the Church: A Study of the Origins of Sectarian Protestantism* (2nd ed., Boston: Starr King, 1958), 229 p.

———: *The Free Church* (Boston: Starr King, 1957), 171 p.

———: "Spiritualizers, Anabaptists and the Church," *Mennonite Quarterly Review,* XXIX (1955), pp. 34-43.

T. W. Manson: *Ministry and Priesthood: Christ's and Ours. Two Lectures* (Richmond: John Knox, 1958), 76 p.

E. L. Mascall: *Christ, the Christian and the Church: A Study of the Incarnation and Its Consequences* (New York: Longmans, Green and Co., 1946), 257 p.

Duke K. McCall, ed.: *What Is the Church: A Symposium of Baptist Thought* (Nashville: Broadman Press, 1958), 189 p.

Geddes MacGregor: *Corpus Christi: The Nature of the Church According to the Reformed Tradition* (Phila.: Westminster, 1958), 302 p.

Ph.-H. Menoud: "Church," *A Companion to the Bible,* J. H. von Allmen, ed. (New York: Oxford Univ. Press, 1958) (also published by Lutterworth Press, London, in 1958 as *Vocabulary of the Bible*).

Donald G. Miller: *The Nature and Mission of the Church* (Richmond: John Knox, 1957), 134 p. (also published at London, England, in 1957 by S.C.M. Press, under the title, *The People of God*).

Paul S. Minear: *Jesus and His People* (New York: Association Press, 1956), 93 p.

——: *Horizons of Christian Community* (St. Louis: Bethany, 1959), 127 p.

——: *Images of the Church in the New Testament* (Phila.: Westminster, 1960), 294 p.

T. Ralph Morton, *The Household of Faith, an Essay on the Changing Pattern of the Church's Life* (Iona Community, Glasgow, 1951).

The Nature of the Church. Papers presented at a Study Conference, Sept. 24, 25, 1958 (Scottdale: Mennonite General Conference, 1958), 88 p., mimeographed.

J. R. Nelson: *The Realm of Redemption: Studies in the Doctrine of the Nature of the Church in Contemporary Protestant Theology* (Greenwich, Conn.: Seabury, 1951), 249 p.

Lesslie Newbigin: *The Household of God.* Lectures on the Nature of the Church (New York: Friendship Press, 1954), 177 p. (also published at London, England, in 1953 by S.C.M. Press).

H. Richard Niebuhr: *The Purpose of the Church and Its Ministry, Reflections on the Aims of Theological Education* (New York: Harper, 1956), 134 p.

Anders Nygren, ed.: *This Is the Church* (Phila.: Muhlenberg, 1952), 353 p.

——: *Christ and His Church* (Phila.: Westminster, 1956), 125 p.

Wilhelm Pauck: "The Idea of the Church in Church History," *Church History,* XXI (1952), pp. 191-213.

Ernest A. Payne: *The Fellowship of Believers; Baptist Thought and Practice Yesterday and Today* (London: Kingsgate, 1944), 110 p.

Robert A. Raines: *New Life in the Church* (New York: Harper, 1951), 155 p.

J. A. T. Robinson: *The Body: A Study in Pauline Theology* (London: S.C.M., 1952), 95 p.

William Robinson: *The Biblical Doctrine of the Church* (St. Louis: Bethany, 1955), 245 p.

Karl Ludwig Schmidt: *The Church (Bible Key Words,* Vol. II, from Gerhard Kittel's *Theologisches Wörterbuch zum Neuen Testament)* (London: Adam and Charles Black, 1950), 75 p. (also published in *Bible Key Words* [New York: Harper, 1955).

Johannes Schneider: *Die Gemeinde nach dem Neuen Testament* (Kassel: Oncken Verlag, 1955), 104 p.

Eduard Schweizer: *Das Leben des Herrn in der Gemeinde und Ihren Diensten: Eine Untersuchung der Neutestamentlichen Gemeindeordnung* (Zürich: Zwingli-Verlag, 1946), 151 p.

——: *Gemeinde und Gemeindeordnung im Neuen Testament* (Zürich: Zwingli-Verlag, 1959), 217 p. (also published by S.C.M. at London in 1961 under the title, *Church Order in the New Testament*).

James D. Smart: *The Rebirth of Ministry: A Study of the Biblical Character of the Church's Ministry* (Phila.: Westminster, 1960), 192 p.

Alan M. Stibbs: *God's Church: A Study in the Biblical Doctrine of the People of God* (Chicago: Inter-Varsity Press, 1959), 128 p.

Studies in Church Discipline, Maynard Shelly, ed. (Newton, Kans.: Mennonite Publication Office, 1958), 241 p.

L. S. Thornton: *The Common Life in the Body of Christ* (Westminster, England: Dacre Press, 1940), 475 p.

T. F. Torrance: *Royal Priesthood.* Scottish Journal of Theology, Occasional Papers No. 3. (Edinburgh: Oliver & Boyd, 1955), 108 p.

——: *Kingdom and Church: A Study in the Theology of the Reformers* (London, Oliver & Boyd, 1956, and Toronto, Clarke, Irwin & Co., Ltd.).

Elton Trueblood: *The Company of the Committed* (New York: Harper, 1961), 113 p.

J. L. Wach: *Church, Denomination and Sect:* Inaugural Lecture (Seabury Western Theological Seminary, 1946), 32 p.

Erland Waltner: "The Anabaptist Conception of the Church," *Mennonite Quarterly Review,* XXV (1951), pp. 5-16.

Robert C. Walton: *The Gathered Community* (London: Carey-Kingsgate, 1946), 184 p.

Claude Welch: *The Reality of the Church* (New York: Scribner's, 1958), 254 p.

INDEXES

INDEX OF NAMES OF PERSONS

INDEX OF SCRIPTURE PASSAGES